Two Teaspoons of Rice

Two Teaspoons of Rice

The Memoir of a Cambodian Orphan

Sida Lei
Monica Boothe

Copyright © 2020 by Sida Lei.
Cover Copyright © 2020 by Sida Lei.
All Rights Reserved.

The scanning, uploading, and distribution
of this book without permission is a theft
of the author's intellectual property.
If you would like permission to use the material
from the book (other than for review purposes),
please contact:
https://TwoTeaspoonsOfRice.com/contact/

First Edition: April 2020

Print book interior design
by Bonnie Burkhardt.

Library of Congress Cataloging-in-publication
Data has been applied for.

ISBN: 978-1-7348528-0-6 (paperback)
978-1-7348528-1-3 (hardcover)
978-1-7348528-2-0 (EPUB)

Printed in the United States of America

Table of Contents

Prologue	1
1. One Family. One Song.	5
2. Like Links in a Chain	25
3. The End of Games	33
4. Protected from the Wind	43
5. Angka's Children	51
6. Where the Water Kept on Flowing	59
7. Why Are You Still Alive?	73
8. In Exchange for This	79
9. To Keep the Light from Slipping Out	83
10. The Question I Couldn't Answer	95
11. The Thought Behind My Tears	101
12. The Other Side of the Mango Trees	109
13. The Moment the Waiting Began	117
14. The Last Place I Was Someone's Daughter	129
15. No Way Out	139
16. They Are Already Dead	149
17. What Hope Sounds Like	155
18. At Last We Were Five	165
19. Someone Who Would Hear Me	169
20. Enough Sunshine in Me	175
21. What We Don't Need	179
22. There He Is Again	183
23. The Answer to the Question	193
24. A Girl Who Had Escaped Again	201

25. Never Again	211
26. Danger in the Rice Paddies	217
27. Like Mist into Rain	227
28. Five Links in a Chain	235
29. The Reason I Was Alive	243
Epilogue	251
Acknowledgements	263

To all the Families at Saint Margaret Mary Church, Rochester, New York

    You gave us hope, freedom and opportunity. You helped us with basic safety living skills at home and in public. You spent your valuable time to set up a home for us and provided furniture, beds, desks, tables, and chairs. Moreover, you shared your family time tutoring us over many months.

    You made medical and dental appointments for five orphans and took us to all those appointments. You sheltered us and supported us. You provided for all our physical, emotional, and spiritual needs.

    Most of all, you taught us how to become good citizens of the United States of America.

I didn't know
if there was a God.
If there was,
I didn't know
His name.

But I knew
that if somebody
didn't help us,
my siblings and I
would die.

Prologue

In Cambodia, we have a saying: you can cut the grass above the ground, but rain will fall, winds will blow, and it will come back alive. If you want it gone - really, truly forever gone, you have to dig out the root. That's exactly what the Khmer Rouge tried to do. It wasn't enough to kill us. They had to dig up our roots.

The year that I turned ten, the Khmer Rouge took over my country. They tore us away from our home and swept the nation clean of everything familiar. They called it Year Zero. The year of nothing. The year it was all cleared away. The year they would start over. The year I first saw death. And oh! did I see death. I saw it in the streets of the city. I saw it in the rice fields. I saw it on the roads between one labor camp and another. I saw it in the mass graves. There was not enough dirt in Cambodia to cover it all. I saw it on the faces of those whom I had never known. And I saw it slip over the eyes of those whom I knew very well. Whom I loved. But the worst of all was the death that came unseen. The death we never really knew for certain, not until years and years later. They never came back. We kept wondering, kept looking, kept hoping, but after enough time had passed, we knew. We knew death had come; still we would always wonder how it had come and when and where.

For four years the Khmer Rouge ruled Cambodia, and death ruled by its side. After four years, when the Khmer Rouge finally fell, the world tried to count. Like me, they wondered and hoped. People tried to put together the pieces, to understand the shape of

Prologue

death in those four years. Their measurements of death varied wildly. 800,000? 1 million? 2 million? 3 million? Somewhere in between. The answer was a quarter of the population. About one in four Cambodians died during those four years.

For my family, the toll was even greater. Before death and the Khmer Rouge stormed into Phnom Penh, we were a family of nine. By the end of those four years, they had whittled us down to five. And like the rest of the world, I would spend the subsequent years counting. Recalculating. Looking. Hoping. Waiting for the numbers to change.

It was two years into the reign of the Khmer Rouge when the waiting started for me. Everything before builds up to this one moment. And everything after comes tumbling down, surging forward under its weight, momentum building – all because of that one moment, the moment when the waiting began. I was twelve-years-old, and I was working in a labor camp. I had spent the last twelve hours working in the rice fields, but the day was over, and we had all gathered in the communal kitchen for our supper. I had been served a bowl of rice like every other child there, and like every other child, I had eaten it eagerly. It was not enough. I was just finishing my last grain of rice, leaving none to save, when a boy came up to me. I didn't know his name, but I'd seen him before. The boy didn't look at me; his eyes kept shifting around, watching for the Mei Kong. That's how I knew there was trouble. He stepped close enough for me to hear him whisper. "I just came back from home," he said. "Did you know that three days ago, they called fourteen men to a meeting? One of them was your dad." *So what?* I wondered. *Angka called for meetings all the time.* "They never came back," the boy

Prologue

whispered. "It's not good." And then he slipped away before the Mei Kong could see.

That was a moment that changed everything. But you won't be able to understand what it changed. You won't know what was lost. Not unless I start from the beginning. Not unless I tell you what I was like before.

Chapter 1

One Family. One Song.

My story begins three years earlier, back when I was still a child. Carefree. Sliding down the spiral banister with my brother and sister. I would start on the fourth floor by our front door. It was a gentle ride at first, down the smooth cement, but at the third floor I'd pick up speed. Thy and Kann would be whipping down after me, but Chao was still up at the top, straining to pull himself onto the cement rail. By the second floor, the air was whipping through my hair, and I was whirling down the coil to the bottom. At the end, I flew off the curved tip and landed on my feet. Thy and Kann came right behind me, their cries of delight punctuating the city air. Then Chao would come running down the steps as fast as his little feet could bring him, determined to catch up, but we were out the door before he could.

The Phnom Penh sunshine came tumbling down to meet us and with it the scrumptious steam billowing from the restaurant next door. Under the fragrance of chicken, onion, cilantro, and browned garlic, our friends were playing. They gathered around a chalk square, a Sprite can at the center. One little boy wound back his arm and hurled forward a flip-flop. It struck the can, which spun out of the square and landed on its side against the wall. I cheered as the boy gleefully gathered his new pile of marbles – the spoil of the game. But I wasn't here to watch their game. I had a message to deliver. "Cock fight at six o'clock!" I called. "Up on the roof!" They all turned to me with eager eyes, and I bounded off across the street.

"Cock fight at six!" I said to my friends who stood in front of the bicycle shop watching the repairman mend their tire. I skipped along to some kids down the street who were swatting a birdie back and forth with their badminton rackets. "Cockfight at six on the roof!" I called, ducking beneath the birdie's arc.

I didn't return to our building until I'd told all the kids on the street. By then, Chao had caught up with us, his eyes wide and his cheeks flushed. "Bong Sida, I can help!" he said.

"I'm thirsty," Kann said. "Get me a glass of water."

Chao nodded and scrambled up the stairs before I could stop him.

"Kann!" I chided, swatting at him, only half-playful. "Don't mistreat our little brother!" Kann smiled impishly as he followed me up the stairs.

When we kicked off our shoes in the living room of the apartment, Chao was already coming down the hall from the kitchen, carefully carrying a glass of water. Kann eagerly took it in his hands and lifted it to his lips. It did look cool and refreshing. Chao smiled at his success in pleasing our brother, two little dimples puckering his round cheeks. My throat was dry after all that running and shouting, and the sound of Kann gulping swallow after swallow was making me even thirstier, and even though the smell of simmering rice drifted down the hall, I hesitated to go near it.

In the end, my thirst won out. I tip-toed into the kitchen. My mother stood over the simmering rice, her thin blouse –white littered with hundreds of tiny yellow daisies—draped against her back, delicate as a flower

One Family. One Song.

petal. The sunshine poured into the kitchen in generous folds, draping itself against my mother's graceful posture. She was beautiful, even in the wafting steam of rice. Little Peou sat at her feet, the fabric of our mother's capris fluttering just above her head. She held her doll in her arms, its stiff plastic form so lifeless against her warm, pudgy frame. My big sister Hong stood next to them in her pressed dress, the color of the sky, its perfect pleats folding the sunlight into straight lines. She was chopping a chicken with swift and precise movements.

I crept toward the sink and reached for a glass, the rhythmic thuds of Hong's knife providing good cover for any sound that might slip through. But when I turned on the faucet and the hiss of water plunged into my glass, Hong spun around, her knife pointed at me. "Sida!" she snapped, and I turned the faucet off again. "Come help with dinner. I need you to chop these onions."

I dropped the glass in the sink and sprang out of the room before she could catch me. "Sida!" I could hear her calling behind. "Can you just help for once?!" But I was already half-way up the stairs to the roof. Hong would never chase me, and even if she did, she was no match for my speed.

Up on the roof, there was no shelter from the sun, but there was plenty of open space, room to run, freedom to shout, and no one to tell me to do any chores.

A blur of white and blue whizzed past. It was my big brother, Chun. I watched him pedal around the roof, tracing the square perimeter that bordered our city block, his white shirt bright in the sunlight. As he started to come back around, I began jumping and waving my hands.

He slowed to a stop in front of me. "Can I ride?" I asked.

One Family. One Song.

    He gave me a smile and a nod, and I climbed onto the rear rack and held onto his shoulders. He started slow, gliding in serpentine curls around the roof. I could feel every curve. His shoulders would shift the slightest bit to the right, and then the whole bike would follow in an outward arc until he shifted back to the left. I was good at holding on, my feet firm on the lower bar, my legs tight against the stays. Slowly I lifted my hands until they were spread as wide as they could go, my fingers splayed to the sun, the wind galloping across my skin.

    But then he started to speed up. I could tell at first because his body would rise, from sitting to standing, and I knew to reach forward and hold tight. This time I gripped him around the waist. "Hold on!" he said, and I could hear the smile in his voice even through the thundering wind. I held on as tight as I could, and he went faster, the world rushing by. "Not so fast!" I cried, but he laughed and picked up speed. Pressed against his back, my arms as tight around him as they could be, my body moved with his. When he turned to the right, I did too, slicing through the air, and then to the left. The world seemed to curl around us. We were flying.

    Then he began to slow down. Slowly I loosened my grip on my brother. At the other end of the roof, Chao was watching us, jumping up and down. Suddenly, Chun slammed on the breaks and swerved to the right. But I was ready. I held tight to his shirt and gripped the bike with my feet. I swung to the side, but I didn't fall.

    Chun laughed. "I almost got you, there."

    "No, you didn't!" I said, and he began to pedal again.

    We stopped in front of Chao. "Let me on," he was saying, reaching for the bike.

One Family. One Song.

I didn't want to get off, so I reached down to help him onto my lap. Chao grinned and climbed up onto my legs. Planting his little feet firmly on my thighs, Chao stood up between Chun and me. I wrapped my arms around Chun's shoulders, firmly pinning our little brother between us. We began to glide forward. Chao squealed with delight, pressing his palms against Chun's head. Giggling, Chao began to steer the bike with our brother's head, turning it to the left and then to the right. Chun would oblige, guiding the bike in the direction of his head.

"Go faster," Chao said. This, too, Chun obliged. As we picked up speed, Chao clung tighter with his little fingers, and I held tighter with my arms. Then suddenly Chun called out "Hold on tight!" as if we could hold any tighter. He swung sharply to the left, and we all tilted towards the ground. "Oh no! We're falling!" Chun cried in feigned fear. Chao let out a gurgling scream but held tight. Chun pulled the bike back upright and resumed his slow pedaling.

"It's fun!" Chao cried. "Do it again!"

When we had made a few laps, Chun slowed to a stop. It was time to go downstairs for supper.

"So, who's coming to the fight?" Chun asked me as we gathered at the bathroom sink to wash our hands.

"Everyone!" I said proudly.

Chun smiled down at me and mussed my windblown hair with his damp palm.

In the hall, my mother had spread out the dinner mat, and Hong was carrying the food in from the kitchen. Stir fry, rice, soup, one by one she set them out on the mat. My family, all nine of us, we sat on the floor in front of our empty plates. The moment my father took his place at the mat, we dug in. I was ladling myself some soup. Kann was piling as much rice on his plate as he could fit. The room filled with the clink of spoons against porcelain, the squish of chicken settling in on a bed of rice, lips slurping up broth, mouths filled with food. There was no time for talking till the food was almost gone.

"So," my father said when his plate was empty. "What's happening? Chun?" He turned to my older brother.

"Cock fight tonight!" Chun said with a grin and served himself a second plate of rice.

"Chao?"

My father turned to my youngest brother whose dimples popped back onto his face. "Oh, I had fun!" he said.

Next was Kann who was only a year older than Chao. "On the way home from school, I bought a cupcake." Kann reported proudly. "It was so yummy!"

"How about you, Peou?" My father asked, even though Peou was the youngest and too little to say much.

She smiled and held up her doll. "Played!" she declared.

"Thy?"

Thy's answer was simple. "I had a good day."

"And you, Hong? What did you do today?"

My big sister sat up straight. "Oh, you know. School, and then I helped Ma with the dinner."

"Sida?" When my father turned my way, I wanted to tell him everything I'd done that day, but there was no way to fit it all in, so I had to stick with the highlights. "I won twenty rubber bands during lunch break!" He smiled, but before I could tell him all about *how* I won them, my mother spoke.

One Family. One Song.

"Yes, *this* one is always playing." She was pointing at me and her face was stern, but there was a smile in her voice. "Never helping with her chores."

"Yeah!" Hong chimed in.

I looked down at my plate. What could I say? It was true.

"And Chun, too!" My mother said. "How can he have time for his homework when he's always off on his bike?"

The dishes were all empty now, so we began to gather them in piles to carry to the kitchen.

"He *can't!*" my mother continued as she handed Chun a stack of dirty plates.

Chun chuckled as he carried them into the kitchen.

"Sida," Hong said, as I set the rice bowl beside the sink. "Help me wash these." But it was almost six o'clock. I ignored her and ran to my bed. I pulled from beneath it a little paper box - my treasure - and, clutching it to my chest, followed Chun up the stairs.

The sun was sinking in the horizon and had left the sky a gentle blue with an equally gentle kind of warmth. Nothing like the blazing heat from earlier. There was already a crowd gathering over by the chicken coop. Chun was kneeling on the roof. He drew two squares with white chalk. Immediately the kids flocked around him just like the chickens they carried. They dropped their treasures into one of the two squares until each was filled with ropes of rubber bands and glistening marbles. I opened my box and added a few treasures of my own to the pile.

"Sida," Chun said, as he rose and dusted his hands on his shorts. "Get the rooster."

One Family. One Song.

"Red Nose?" I asked. Red Nose was one of our best fighters, but he had been the last to fight and might have needed some rest. Chun was always the one to decide.

"Yin-and-Yang," Chun said.

I ran to our coop. Our four chickens were meandering back and forth behind the wooden slats. I stepped in, grabbed the black one with the black-and-white speckled comb, and carried him out. As I closed the door, there was a tug on my shirt. Chao was smiling up at me. "I can help," he said. "I can hold the chicken." He held his arms out as if to demonstrate that they were big enough. It was true that it would be hard for me to keep track of the bets for Chun while holding the rooster, and Yin-and-Yang was calm enough –when he wasn't fighting that is—so I carefully placed him in my little brother's arms. But Chao strained to hold the feathery body. He hugged the chicken desperately to his chest.

"No, Chao," I said. "You hold it out on your forearm, like this." I demonstrated, stretching my own arm out under an imaginary chicken. But Chao could barely move his arms without dropping the bird. I laughed. "Never mind, Chao," I said, taking the rooster back. "Just come with me."

When we got back, I began to count the rubber bands and marbles in the chalk squares. It was my job to keep track of them during the fight. I was almost finished when Chun took Yin-and-Yang from my arms and carried him into the middle of the crowd. It was time for him to meet his opponent. Chun would hold him and swing him back and forth toward the other chicken until he was angry. Then he would set Yin-and-Yang on the ground so that he and the other rooster could go at each other, but I was missing all of this because I was in

One Family. One Song.

charge of the betting. There was an eruption of cheers, and I knew the fight had begun.

"I can watch this spot," Chao offered, his dimples back with his smile.

"Okay," I said, patting him on the head, and I pushed my way into center of the crowd. I found a place and sat down next to Thy and Kann right in the front. Yin-and-Yang was charging at a red-feathered chicken. "Go! Yin-and-Yang!" they cried, and I joined them. "Go!" When the rooster unleashed a flurry of talons at the red one, we cheered. This was going to be one of our better fights. "Get him!" I shouted, and as if in response, Yin-and-Yang lunged for the other rooster with his beak. A boy hurried in to pull the red rooster out of the fight. We had won! The air was thick with feathers, black, white, and red. They floated through the air like confetti. I pushed back through the crowd to the chalk squares where Chao was patiently watching them. Those who had bet on Yin-and-Yang were here to gather their prize. Carefully, I counted out the right number to each of my friends. I was the last to gather mine. A beautifully thick wad of rubber bands. I gently tucked it into my box.

It was starting to get dark now. The sun was on the horizon, and the sky was fiery with color. Most of the kids had gone home and the roosters were back in their coops. I sat down and opened up the box in my lap. It would take me a while to attach the new rubber bands to ones I already had in my rope, but I didn't mind. It was one of my favorite things to do.

When the sun had vanished and darkness spread across the sky, I closed my box and carried it downstairs.

"Sida!" I heard my father's voice coming from the living room. He was laying on a cushion on the floor. Thy sat at his side, leaning down over his head, her

One Family. One Song.

fingers searching through his hair. I knew exactly what she was looking for. "You're just in time," my father said. "Come help your sister."

I bounded over and began to pick through his thick hair with my fingers. Ever since he had started to go gray, he had asked Thy and me to do this. "Found one!" Thy cried. Pinched between her thumb and index finger was a long silver hair. I helped her, pushing away the other black hairs around it so that we could see down to the skin of his scalp while she reached in with the tweezers and plucked it. "One!" I announced. Thy gently laid it on the bed, and we resumed our hunt for the gray hairs. We counted each aloud as we plucked it. "Two!" "Three!" "Four!" Once, Thy accidentally slipped and the hair that sprang out between her tweezers was black. Her eyes grew wide, and she bit her lip, but I covered for her. "Five!" I declared proudly, and quietly took the hair from her, shoving it into my pocket. We went right back to looking for gray hairs.

When we plucked our last, Thy and I called out in unison, "Ten!" We held out the thin clump of gray hairs, and our father smiled, patting us each on our heads. Then he reached into his pocket and pulled out 1 riel for each of us. "Thank you, Pa!" I cried and tucked the little coin next to my rubber band rope in my box.

That night, I climbed up the ladder to my bed. Thy was already nestled in under the sheets, and I lay down next to her. Hong turned off the light. I could hear the creak of her mattress as she climbed into bed with Peou just below us. The quiet whirring of the fan whispered cool air across our skin. Even through its sound, I could hear Kann and Chao's hushed voices from the bed they shared on the other side of the room. I was

One Family. One Song.

thinking about my growing rubber band collection and the new riel in my box. It had been a good day.

"Bong Sida," Thy's whisper interrupted my thoughts. "What are we going to do tomorrow?" I had to think. What wouldn't we do tomorrow? We could ride our bikes. Go watch Chun play in a ping pong tournament? Ask Pa to take us to a movie? Play badminton? Kick the can? Another cock fight? Play hide-and-go-seek? Take the chickens for a walk on the roof? Anything. We could do anything.

"Have fun." I told her at last. That was the one thing I knew for sure that we would do.

"Okay," Thy said, and the teeth of her smile shone faintly in the moonlight.

The next morning, when I came running into the kitchen for breakfast, Hong was lighting the incense on our ancestral shrine. Our mother had set out a fresh bowl of fruit for our ancestors, and Hong stood before it reverently and prayed for peace and good fortune. Her prayers rose up in a tiny thread of smoke that dissolved into the air and drifted away. Invisible or gone? It was impossible to know for sure.

At least this meant she couldn't tell me to help her clean or wash up. I cut a thick slice of bread from the baguette on the counter and opened a can of sweetened condensed milk. The milk poured onto my plate in thick folds. At the table, I dipped my bread into the milk and put it to my mouth, sucking out all the creamy sweetness. When the milk was gone, I still had plenty of bread, so I looked around. No one was there to see. Quickly I poured myself a second puddle of milk and dipped in. When the bread was gone, I licked and licked at the plate until there wasn't a hint that the milk had ever been there.

My mother came through the room - a blur of pink, so quick, so graceful, you almost weren't sure she'd been there. Like a breeze of plumeria petals the wind swept through the room and was gone. She had deposited Peou on the floor beside me and gone off to help my little brothers get ready. I gave the plate one last lick and got down on the floor to play with Peou. When I tickled her stomach, she giggled, and her mouth opened in a crooked smile. Then I pulled her onto my back and crawled on my hands and knees into the living room. Her little fingers gripping tight onto my shoulders, I swayed back and forth, each sway accompanied by a delighted squeal from Peou.

Before long, Chao was at our side, dressed in a school uniform and bobbing up and down, one dimple on each side of his smile. Chao was too young for school, but he dressed himself in a uniform anyway so he could pretend to be like the rest of us. "Let me on! Let me on!"

"Okay," I said, reaching behind me to pull Peou from my back. She found her doll and settled comfortably in the corner to watch. I knelt down again, and Chao climbed onto my back. Chao was much bigger, and his arms could reach all the way around my neck for a secure grip, so he could handle a much wilder ride. I galloped across the living room floor till my knees and palms ached. I reared up like a wild stallion, swung sharply from side to side, dropped suddenly to my stomach, and made dramatic turns to try to hurl him from my back. But every time, Chao clung with a tenacious grip, his laughter and screams bubbling out like a pot of rice boiling over.

One Family. One Song.

When I made one last twist in an attempt to sling him off the side and onto the rug, his arms tightened around my neck so much I could barely breathe. "Okay, stop! Stop!" I wheezed. "You have to let go, Chao." His little arms released, and he climbed down. Even through his disappointment, the smile and its accompanying dimples shone.

Kann was trying to climb onto my back then. He was a little bigger than Chao and his feet touched the ground. "Kann, you're too big for this!" I tried to crawl to the other side of the room, his feet dragging along the floor. "Ok, you're not riding again," I told him when I reached the other side. He climbed off reluctantly.

"Kids, go to school!" My father's voice snipped through the air. It wasn't loud, but it was stern, and we knew it was meant to be obeyed. Immediately, we were on our feet and scrambling out the door.

"Sida! Your clothes!" Hong called out as she slung her book bag over her shoulder and headed out behind me. I looked down at my uniform. My button-down shirt and my navy skirt were clean, but they hung on my body in a rumpled mass, unlike Hong's skirt and blouse which were crisp and straight.

"You didn't fold them, Bong Hong, remember?" I called back. Hong had gotten so fed up with my repeated failure to help her with the laundry, that the last time she'd done it, she'd folded everyone's clothes but mine, which she'd handed to me in a giant wad. I had shoved the wad into my drawer and gone biking with Thy.

"That's because *you* were supposed to fold them." Hong flung her hands into the air with exasperation.

I just shrugged and hurried on ahead of her.

One Family. One Song.

After school, Thy, Kann, and I raced back home to see who could get to our bikes first. I won, of course, charging into the house so fast that I almost knocked my mother over. She had been standing with Peou near the doorway and had to dodge me with a swift twist of her hips and a careful rebalancing on her toes. Her pink skirt swayed back and forth. "Careful, Sida!" she chided as I hurried out of my shoes. She reached for me to press her lips against my cheek. The smell of soap wafted about her.

"Sida!" she cried as she pulled away from me. "Go take a shower! You stink!" I was covered in a thin film of sweat that had caked with dust. "And after that, help your sister make dinner."

"Okay, Ma." I hurried off, not to the bathroom, but to my bike. Before long, the wind was in my hair, on my skin, and cries of "Wait for us, Bong Sida!" coming from Kann and Thy trailed behind me, the sound of my victory. I was winning!

But after a while, I was bored with beating Kann and Thy. They were, after all, both younger than me. So I left them on the roof and went to find Chun. He was in the living room, drawing. "Bong Chun, want to go ride?" I asked with my most winning smile.

But he didn't even look up. "Not now, Sida."

"Want to do something else? Ping pong? Anything?"

"No."

So I sat down across from him and waited patiently as he sketched careful lines across the paper with his pencil, curled perfect arcs with his metal compass. When he got up to get a glass of water, I seized

One Family. One Song.

my opportunity. I grabbed the compass and sprang out the door.

When I came back into the living room, Chun stood with his hands on his hips looking around. "Have you seen my compass, Sida?" he asked, still scanning the room.

"I know where it is," I said, holding my hands behind my back and swaying gentle like the breeze. "What will you give me if I bring it to you?"

Chun looked down at me. He was trying to look stern, but there was a smile hiding behind those firm, straight lips. "What do you want?"

"Some candy?"

He pressed his lips together as if to lock in a laugh. "Okay, bring it."

I went rushing out to retrieve his compass. When I came back, he had a handful of hard candy ready. I was just reaching for it when I heard my mother's voice.

"Sida!" I flinched at the sharpness with which she pronounced my name. "I told you an hour ago to help your sister with the soup. She's in there cooking alone, and I see now that you haven't showered either, as I told you." Silently, Chun slipped back to his drawing and out of her line of wrath. "Come here."

I dropped the candy into my pocket and approached her slowly. I tried to think of something I could say. Some excuse, some compliment, something to get me out of this, but my mind was blank.

My mother lifted up a long stick and spoke quietly. "Give me your hand." I held it out, my mind still whirling. What could I say? How could I stop this? She raised the stick. With a whir, it arced towards my hand, but before it could strike, I pulled my hand back. I turned and ran.

One Family. One Song.

Everything could be solved running. No one could catch me – not Hong, not my mother. "Come back here now!" She called from the doorway, but I was halfway down the stairs. "Come back here, Sida! Come back!" But I was almost out of the building. "When you come back, you will get even more whips than you would have!" But I was gone.

I found some friends to play with. Joined a game of badminton. Watched a round of ping pong at the gym. But as the sky grew dim and the air cooled, I knew I had to go home.

When I came into the apartment, the smell of soup permeated the house. Hong was setting bowls out on the mat. I stepped in quietly, but my mother heard me anyway. She turned and looked at me, her head tilted to the side, like a flower bent in the breeze. "Come here, Sida," she said, reaching for her stick. I held my hand out. "How many times should I whip you?" she asked.

"Ten." I spoke quietly.

"You ran away, so what is your punishment?"

"Ten."

"No, you get twenty."

I wanted to counter-offer. To give some good reason why it should be less. But I had nothing to say. She flicked the stick against my hand. Once. Twice. Twenty times. But it was a slight sting. Not so hard as it would have been if she had whipped me before, when she was still angry. I decided that I had won after all.

After dinner, we all went up onto the roof. The moon was full that night, and its light plunged down toward us. My father pulled out his harmonica and, putting it to his lips, flung a song into the moon-drenched sky. At first, we just listened to him play. Listened to

One Family. One Song.

the music, along with the night, spreading itself across the city. But after a while, we couldn't let him keep making that music alone. We joined in. One by one our voices layered themselves with the harmonica, until we were all singing. One family. One song.

That night, after Hong had turned off the lights, and our room was dark, Thy had fallen asleep, and Chao and Kann's whispers had faded into the soft sounds of breathing. I noticed a faint light coming through the curtains that hung between our side of the bedroom and our brothers'. I crept down the ladder, pushed aside the floral curtain, and climbed up to the top bunk of my brothers' bed. Chun lay on his back, a tiny lamp shining upon the pages of his paperback novel. I stretched out on the sheets next to him. Even at his side I could feel the slight rise and fall of his breath.

"Bong Chun," I whispered.

But he said nothing. He turned the page.

"What should we do tomorrow?" I asked.

"Tomorrow we're going to Grandma's," he whispered back.

"We are?"

But his eyes were on the book.

"For how long?"

He turned the page again. "Just the weekend."

I was quiet for a while, trying to think of something to say. Something to lure him from the book. In the end I could think of nothing. So I just poked him. Then again. Not hard. Just enough to annoy.

He swatted at my hand with a book, but he was laughing quietly.

"Bong Chun," I whispered.

He put down the book at last.

One Family. One Song.

"When Thy and I were plucking Pa's gray hairs…"

"Mmmhmm…"

"I counted ten, but really we only pulled eight."

"Sida!" he chided. "Don't do that! You could get in trouble if he catches you!"

I knew this, but it wasn't getting in trouble that worried me. I thought about my father, the way his eyes closed when he played the harmonica, the times he'd taken me to the movies. He'd taken all of us kids many times, but I was thinking of the times that he took just me. And all the times he'd taken me to the gym to watch him play in ping pong tournaments. The way he would look at me and grin when he had won a match. I thought of the many hours I had spent in his work room watching him make jewelry. He would use his tools to take a bar of gold and pull from it a slender thread. This thread he would spin into a coil and then cut into hundreds of little tiny links. Each one so small and fragile that by itself it was nothing, but when it was joined with others like it, a chain, it became beautiful, valuable. I remembered my father letting me press the links closed with my own little fingers. Then he would take the chain from me and seal it with the gas torch. At the touch of fire, the links clung to each other with a new-found permanence. I thought of glint of light when he laid a newly coiled chain in my hand so I could see.

But Chun reached up his hand and ruffled my hair with his palm, and I knew it was okay. So I curled up next to him and let the world slowly slip away.

In the morning, I was back in my bed. Chun had woken me and sent me back during the night. The sun was streaming in bright through the windows. *We are*

One Family. One Song.

going to Grandma's today! After breakfast, we all ran out the door to the car. My father was folding back its canvas roof. Chun, Hong, and I slipped into the back first, then Kann, Chao, and Peou squeezed in on our laps. My father started the engine and we rumbled our way down the street. As we picked up speed, the wind surged across us, blowing the city farther and farther away. We stretched out our arms into its gusts. Then my father burst into song, his voice whipping along with the wind. And we all joined in. Together, we threw our voices into the sky. All the world tumbling by with the wind, there was nothing in the world besides us. My family.

Chapter 2

Like Links in a Chain

That was the way it was for a long time. Simple. Happy. Just me and my family. But everything changed when I was ten. The change came with a whistle, gentle at first, then louder. It faded out, but then a crash shook the whole building like an earthquake.

It was the first time I heard a bomb. I'd known that there was war. I'd heard about the fighting in the countryside and the word "communism," which whispered its name across these rumors, but I didn't know the growing threat. I didn't know that the war in neighboring Vietnam had bled over our borders steadily for years, that the Communists of North Vietnam established bases and supply lines throughout Cambodia, and that Communists in my own country had aided them. I didn't know that our Prime Minister Lon Nol had allied with the Americans who had been bombing Communists across our country for months. And I certainly didn't know that the Americans were pulling out the very last troops from Vietnam, as well as the last of their citizens from my own country. I didn't know that the city in which I lived was the war prize of the nation, the last bastion, the final piece necessary to birth Communist Cambodia. No, I thought the war was a distant and muffled thing, like a quiet hum in the background. But when the bombs came to Phnom Penh, my world was shattered, too.

The second bomb came just behind the first. And then a third. One after another they fell upon the city.

Like Links in a Chain

From every direction, we came running. Hong from the kitchen, I from the bedroom, my father from his workroom. Chao was crying. Peou whimpered into my mother's shoulder. We gathered together in the corner of the living room. I pressed in against the legs of my mother, Chao nestled on one side, Thy on the other. All nine members of the Kong family bundled together. Every time a bomb landed, we - along with the rest of the city - shuddered.

"What is it?" Kann whispered, as though the bombs could hear us, as though we could hide from them.

"Bombs," Chun said, his voice also hushed.

And another one whistled over our heads and then exploded somewhere nearby.

Then they stopped. It was quiet for a while. Then the bombs returned. Even when it was quiet, we were scared to leave the safety of our brothers' and sisters' warmth. So we stayed there together until darkness fell, and then we curled up against one another and slept. We stayed that way for nearly two weeks. Huddled together in the living room.

Sometimes the city was quiet, smoke and dust wafting in through the windows. My mother would steal away to the kitchen and return with some canned sardines or some dried sausages. Chun would ask if he could go outside. "No. Nobody go outside," my father said, his voice firm. So we sat in a tangle together, reading, playing quietly.

And sometimes the bombs came back, sang their way across the sky, and then belched destruction onto the neighboring buildings. When we heard their high-pitched roar overhead, we clutched each other's hands in fear, but what we came to realize was that the whistling

Like Links in a Chain

sound meant safety. It meant the bomb was passing over. If a bomb were ever to crash into our home, we wouldn't hear it singing first. I looked up at the ceiling above us. Since we lived on the top floor, the layer between us and the bomb-riddled sky was so thin.

When a bomb hit nearby, we could see its breath. It rose up in a dark cloud of smoke of dust. From where I sat, I could see it through the window.

"Who's dropping the bombs?" Hong whispered. "And who are they aiming for?" But that was a question no one would answer.

After the tenth day, the city fell quiet. The sky was empty and the ground still. We waited for the whistle overhead, but it never came.

Just as the sound of a bomb whistling overhead meant safety, the silence that followed meant danger. Something worse was barreling towards us, and we would not hear it. We would not know until long after it had struck what a terrible thing it was.

Out of the silence came the distant rumble of a truck. Then voices, urgent and sharp, snapping through the streets below. We crept out of our corner to the balcony. Soldiers were swarming through the street, but they were not the soldiers we were used to, with their green uniforms. These men wore simple black clothes, like pajamas. The trucks slowly inched forward, and from their backs sprang the soldiers. The men began banging on the doors they passed. "Get out!" they shouted. "Get out!"

I was just tall enough to see them over the edge of the balcony. Chao tugged at my shirt, and I lifted him up so that he, too could watch. There were some cheers that flickered out from the homes below us, but we were too afraid of the guns on their backs to make a sound.

Like Links in a Chain

The soldiers didn't cheer along. "Get out of the city!" they barked. "The Americans are going to bomb tonight!" One soldier pointed his gun into the air and cracked the sky as he shouted. We all scrambled back into the house.

Then a voice rang out, loud and garbled through a megaphone. "The Americans are going to bomb the city. You must leave the city tonight!"

Even if I had known about the Americans and the war, how could I have known – how could any of us have known – that they were lying? It was perhaps the most genius move of the whole regime. One massive con: to convince an entire city to abandon their homes leaving them wide open for looting.

"Get out! Move! Move!" Their shouts kept coming.

Inside it was a blur. My mother fluttering from room to room, Peou in her arms. My father calling out the window to our neighbors. Our minds whirling. *What are we going to do?*

Then my mother was handing me a bag. "Go pack," she said.

So I did. I gathered two sets of clothes and my favorite books. My mother brought me a quilt, and I stuffed that in as well. I opened the dresser drawer and looked at my treasure box. It was too big, and with all those marbles I knew it would be too heavy. I emptied out my pencil box from my school bag and filled it instead with the shiniest marbles and freshest, most colorful rubber bands. When the box was full, I tucked it deep into my bag. I picked up my piggy bank. *If my parents see this,* I thought, *they'll tell me to break it and pack the money.* But it was my piggy bank. So I hid it in the folds of the quilt and carried my bag out of the living room.

My father lifted the bag with one hand. "Too heavy," he said, peering into it. "Take out the books."

So I went back to my room and removed all but two books. That was all I could bear to leave behind.

Before long we were shuffling out the door, each of us with our bags slung over our shoulders. We stepped into the gleaming sunlight in a long chain, just like the golden chains my father had made. The streets were packed, and rippling like a flooded river. We had to hold hands to keep from getting swept away. I held Thy's hand on one side and Chun's on the other. The air was filled with dust, ash, gasoline fumes, and sweat. As we made our way down the street, slowly the crowds began to thin.

That was when I first saw them, shapes lying down in the street. I craned to get a better look as I walked. *Is that what I think it is?* But through the crowds I couldn't tell for sure. "Don't look," my mother called back to me from where she was walking just ahead. But I wanted to see. I wanted to know. I saw one on my left. He was wearing a green military uniform, but it was wet with the blood that had dripped down from his thick head of hair. He was laying on his side, but the side of his face that I could see was a swollen and splotched, gray and blue. I shuddered and sprang forward to my mom, clutching the fabric of her shirt.

This was the first glimpse I had of death. It was the first of many.

Night fell on the city, and still we were walking. Still clinging to one another as we walked. Still thinking of the ghosts that hovered above the bodies we had

Like Links in a Chain

passed. The crowds were thinner now, and we could walk with more ease.

The sky slowly pieced itself together like a puzzle as, bit by bit, the city fell away behind us. It was a darkened sky-puzzle with only lingering wisps of color to remind us that not long ago the sun had been there. Now there was a new source of light in the distance. A fiery orange surged up ahead. We were walking towards it. It was night, but the more we walked, the warmer and brighter it got. As we drew closer, we could smell it, too, the acrid smoke. It was a gas station burning. We passed within a few hundred feet of the flame, close enough to feel its withering heat, to feel the patter of ash that rained down from the black cloud that billowed overhead. I shook my head and ran my fingers through my hair to chase the ash out of it.

As we walked on in the orange glow of the fire, I saw more corpses on the side of the road, but I didn't want to see anymore. I clung to the collar of little Chao. He was a link in the chain. If I clung to the chain, I wouldn't get lost.

Finally, we stopped. We found a grassy ditch on the side of the road and spread out some sheets on the ground. We lay down in a long row, one next to the other. I chose my spot between Chun and Hong. They were my *bong*, my older brother and sister. Between them I would be safe from ghosts.

The soldiers had said that the Americans would be bombing the city tonight. I waited for the sound of bombs. I heard nothing but the sound of my parents hushed voices, whispering to each other and to the other adults nearby. I didn't want to sleep. I wanted to know what was happening, so silently I crept towards them, but my father saw me. "Go to sleep, Sida," he said. I crawled back to my place between Bong Hong and Bong Chun.

Above me the sky stretched black, strewn with a profusion of white stars. *What's going to happen to us?* I wondered. *What is this world I live in now?* There were no answers to these questions. There were only stars. I began to count them. One, two, three stars. Like links in a chain. Four, five. I got to fifty before I fell asleep.

Chapter 3

The End of Games

When I woke in the morning, the air was chilly, but I was swaddled in the warmth of something soft. For a moment, I thought that something good had happened during the night. Maybe we had found a cozy house and had been invited in. That my parents had carried me to a warm bed, and that was where I was now. A home.

But when I opened my eyes, I saw the dew-glazed grass, my siblings lying by my side, crowds of strangers shuffling on the asphalt next to us. We were still here, on the side of the road. I lifted the quilt that had been spread across me during the night and stood up. My parents stood nearby, talking to some other grownups, their voices quiet and somber. I stood next to my father and took his hand.

"We tried, but they wouldn't let us," another man was saying. "The soldiers forbade it."

"Did they say why?" my father asked.

The man shrugged. "They didn't say anything. They're not telling anyone anything."

My father turned to my mother. "We have to try. Surely, they won't keep us out of our own homes in broad daylight." My mother nodded. "I'll take Chun with me," he said.

"Let me go, too." I said. "I want to come."

"No." My father let go of my hand and went to tell Chun. A moment later, my father and brother were heading down the road back towards our home. I watched them walk away. I watched until I couldn't see them anymore.

When a baker came by with a tub full of bread, my mother bargained with him, shoved a giant wad of money into his hands, and then passed a baguette down the row. We each tore off a piece and ate. When I was finished, my mother called me. "Sida, go with your sister to the well." She handed Hong a large plastic bucket and pointed to a steady stream of people, moving away from the road. "It's somewhere that way. Follow the crowds and bring back some water."

So Hong and I joined the stream, following the feet of strangers before us. When we reached the well, we waited our turn to drop the well's wooden bucket deep into the water. Then Hong pulled the rope to haul it back up and pour its contents into our plastic bucket. We spread some banana leaves on the surface to stabilize the water, a trick taught us by one of the other women in the crowd. Now that it was full, our bucket was far too heavy for Hong to carry alone. With my hand on one side of the handle and her hand on the other, we lifted the bucket off the ground. Slowly we trudged back to the road.

When we made it back to our family, I saw a familiar figure crouched down next to my siblings. It was my friend Ny.

Ny and her family lived two doors down in our apartment building in Phnom Penh. She was my favorite playmate in the neighborhood because she was daring. She liked all the games I liked, rubber bands, marbles, jump rope, racing. She was good at running. Almost as good as me. Once she had even beaten me. After that I started training myself, practicing. I had to become the best again. Ny was fun because she would do

The End of Games

anything... anything but jump from high heights. Ever since that one time we got caught jumping off the roof of our building onto the neighboring roof, she had been afraid of heights.

But for all the fun that Ny was, playing with her was a rare treat. She was the oldest in her family, so like Hong she was always laden with many chores and responsibilities. Unlike Hong, though, she looked for every opportunity to shirk them. Her mom was always sending her younger siblings out with her. They trailed behind her, little animated reminders of what it meant to be "Bong." There was Lane, who was only a few years younger and not too much of a pest, and her younger sister whom we called "Flower Girl" because she always found a pretty flower to tuck into her hair, and then her little brother whom we called "Cry Baby" because that was all he ever seemed to do. But Ny and I, we were experts. We always found some way to distract them and then to sneak off. They were little kids, and Ny and I were runners. They were never able to catch up.

So there sat Ny, and alongside her, Lane, Flower Girl, and Cry Baby. There was no sneaking off now. Not that we wanted to. Everything was different now. There was nothing to do but to sit and wait. Still, if I had to wait, I was glad to have a friend to wait with.

We hadn't been waiting long, when we saw a crowd moving towards us. It was coming from the direction of the city, and it was moving fast. As it drew closer, I could see my father and brother in the crowd. They were running. When they reached us, my father's eyes were wild, and when he spoke his voice was different, not the calm, certain voice I had always known. "We can't get back in!" he told my mother. "We can't get in!"

The End of Games

"But we have nothing." My mother was gesturing around us, the panic slipping from my father's voice into hers. "What will we do?"

"I don't know. I don't know. But we can't get back in. No one can!" He was speaking quickly, his words a jumble.

"Oh no!" I cried, reaching for the hem of my father's shirt. I needed his calm, reassuring voice to come back, to tell me that it would all be all right, that everything would return to normal soon. "Pa, I left a lot of my clothes, my books," I told him. "The chickens are still on the roof." Tears were beginning to spill into my words on onto my cheeks. "What will happen to my books?" I thought of the shelf in the bedroom with all my paperbacks stacked neatly and of all those rubber bands & marbles that I had so diligently earned.

"Be quiet, Sida!" His voice was still not the calm one I craved. "Be quiet. We can't do anything about it!"

And that was when I got scared. I think I knew it was the end. Of course, I didn't know all of it. I didn't know that it was the end of life as a I knew it. I didn't know it was the end of my country, my family. I didn't know it was the end of my childhood. What I did know was that it was the end of games, the end of fun.

A truck had pulled up into the street next to us. Soldiers we later called Khmer Rouge, stood in the back with their guns. One soldier barked orders through the megaphone. "Move! Keep walking!" So we gathered up our bags. "You can't go back to the city," he shouted. "Move forward. Quick." He snapped three bullets into the air, a burst of angry exclamation points. Just as the day before, we began to walk.

Hong and I took turns carrying the bucket. It was only half-full now, but it was still heavy. Whenever we

The End of Games

pleaded with my mother for her to let us empty it out, she shook her head.

We saw them on the sides of the road. Corpses. Most of them were men in military uniforms. "Don't look," my mother would say when she saw them. But it was daytime now, the horror of the last night had passed, and I was curious again. I craned my neck to see. Maybe in their fallen bodies there would be some hint, some clue, to help me understand this world that we were living in now. But they were too far away, I couldn't make out any details, anything to tell me who they were or what had happened.

I was straining so hard to see the corpses in the distance that I didn't see the one right in front of me. I almost tripped over it. The sudden realization of what it was –this thing beneath my foot, this thing that not long ago was alive like me - it shuddered over me, and I ran. I ran to my mother's side, to the familiar hem of her shirt, to its silky comfort on my fingers.

We walked a few more miles that day. We were far from the city now. There were no brick buildings. No cement. Instead we saw the occasional thatched hut, raised on posts a few feet from the ground. But these were few, and between each we saw many trees. Papaya and mango. Tamarind and coconut. And banana trees. We passed so many banana trees, their long flat leaves slick with sunlight. The only thing that stretched farther than the trees was the sky. Blue and blank and endless, flecked with nothing but relentless sunlight. Finally, we stopped. The truck with the soldiers was long gone, and there was no one to tell us we couldn't. There was a farm with a couple of little huts surrounded by fields. It was as good a place as any. So all of us walked to one of the huts - Ny's family, mine, and a few others I didn't know.

The End of Games

Immediately, the grownups got to work. They gathered up what food they could find in the hut and started a fire. My mother and Hong were setting up a pot over the fire. There was no room for us all in the little hut, so we kids lingered outside.

There was nothing to do, and the sun was still hot, even as it leaned towards the western horizon. Then I felt a nudge at my side. It was Ny. She pointed to the hut steps, where some women were carrying a couple of yucca roots into the house. "Let's go find some food," she said.

It was just like old times, sneaking away from our brothers and sisters. Ny and I found a field in the back where some green leafy plants were growing in rows. I'd lived in the city all my life, and I didn't know one crop from another, but whatever was here, it had to be edible. We took a few steps into the field. The ground puffed dry, brown clouds around our feet with each step. There were a lot of empty spaces in the rows of plants, the plant gone and a small hole in its place. It looked like we weren't the first to have the idea to come here looking for food.

"What are these?" I asked, examining the leaves for anything familiar. It didn't look like anything I'd ever eaten before. But then I found one that had been pulled from the ground. It lay on its side in the dust. I lifted it in my hand. From the green stem dangled a scrawny pink root. "They're yams!" I called to Ny, holding up my prize. She took it between her fingers.

"This one's too small," she said, and she was right. It has hardly bigger than my thumb, and not worth the work of cooking it. I dropped it back on the ground, and we began to slowly move down the path between two rows of plants. Ny walked in front, and I right behind. It was like a hunt, examining each plant to see if it had the same kind of leaves as the yam I had found, or if it was a weed. The ones that looked like yams I had to wiggle and twist and then to gently pull in order to keep from breaking the root. But most that I pulled up were like the first. Too small.

Finally, I found one that really resisted the pulling. "I think I found a good one!" I said. Ny knelt beside me, and her fingers joined mine, digging around the root, slowly relieving it of the dirt that held it to the ground. When it finally released its grip from the earth, we pulled it up to see. It was a plump one, stretching all the way across my hand. We looked at each other and smiled. Then we turned back to the hunt.

I was looking into the weeds, wondering if those leaves hiding beneath might be a yam plant, when an explosion knocked me off my feet. The world blinked away for a moment. Then it returned, but it was different from before. The sky was smothered in dust, and I could see nothing but its tiny brown flecks drifting around me. They coated my skin and my hair and my breath. It was silent, too, this drifting world, but in this silence, there was a kind of echo of sound. The memory of it.

Then I could feel the ground beneath me. I was lying on it. I pushed my hands against the earth and stood. The dust was beginning to settle now. I could see little particles of the world underneath it. The blue sky, the yam fields, the green plants, and Ny. Ny was on the ground. She was lying still, but somehow it looked wrong. I blinked. Tried to wipe the dust from my eyes so I could see. Ny was there. The dust covered her like a blanket, almost like she was sleeping, tucked in for the night. But not at all like that. It looked all wrong. I blinked again, my eyelids scraping away a thin layer of dirt.

I realized, then, what was wrong with Ny. She lay at an angle, her feet up on the raised yam beds, her face down on the lower path between rows. I took a step towards her. Her eyes were open, and she blinked, but she didn't say anything. Then her hand reached for mine, fingers stretching toward fingers.

I didn't understand. I couldn't make it make sense.

And then there were grownups there. Several men, I wasn't sure who. My father might have been among them, but I didn't pay attention. I was still trying to figure it out. They were calling out orders. They were lifting her body. They were carrying her back to the hut.

That was when I saw that her foot was gone. As they carried her away, one empty leg dragged along the ground, trailing blood. "Pick up her leg!" One of the men yelled, and someone did, lifting it above the ground. I could see now, that it stopped at the ankle, her skin hanging in ragged shreds around the opening, like the ragged shreds of her pants that hung red and muddy around it. And I watched her eyes, still and dull behind their occasional blink, blink. She was asking the same thing I was. *What happened?*

When they carried her to the hut, all of us kids were sent outside. A man with a doctor's kit hurried into the hut after her. But Lane, Flower Girl, Cry Baby, all of my own brothers and sisters, and me, we all sat on a log and waited. Silence floated about us like the dust, a smothering cloud that we had no choice but to breathe.

It could have been me. I drew the thought in with the air and the silence. *It could have been me.* I breathed

The End of Games

it back out. There was nothing I could do but wait. And breathe.

Many years later, I would ask a land mine expert about this, marveling at how close I had been to the explosion, and yet unscathed. He would tell me that land mines explode vertically, a slender tube of destruction. Ny had been inside that tube, and I had not.

After a while, my mother came out of the hut and sat next to me. She stretched a warm arm around my shoulder and pulled me close. "Don't worry, Sida," she whispered.

"Will she die?" I asked.

"The doctor will try to save her."

I looked at the hut. I couldn't see Ny inside, but I could see shapes, moving back and forth, adults moving around the room. They were trying.

"How are you doing?" she whispered into my ear.

"I'm scared."

My father came out then. He looked into my eyes. "Don't go anywhere alone, Sida. You understand?" I nodded.

Then they both went back in the hut.

And we waited.

It was while we were waiting that the soldiers came. They rumbled up in their truck. "You can't stay here!" their megaphone boomed. "Move on! Move on!"

Around us, people started packing up. They gathered up their belongings and trudged on down the road. But we stayed.

The sun began to set. I watched darkness fall on the hut where Ny lay. In the fading light, a shape stepped into the doorway. "She has passed," a voice said.

The End of Games

　　I remember her mother and father, shaking with tears. Everyone around us was in tears. But behind all the tears, the men got to work right away. They wrapped her in a mat, dug a hole beneath her in the dirt floor of the hut, laid her inside it, and they piled it back high in a mound. We had a moment of silence. Someone said some comforting words, but I don't remember them.

　　We picked up our bags. It was dark by now. We walked away in darkness.

Chapter 4

Protected from the Wind

A couple days later, the Khmer Rouge sent us to live in a valley that was surrounded by tall, green mountains. At night, a thick, chilly fog would cling to the air well into the morning. It was in this fog that we built our first house. We were given a few days and some machetes to clear the land of its wild grass that grew high over our heads. My siblings and I used these grass blades to weave a roof for the house, while the grownups cut the trees that would become the six posts to hold up that roof. We made piles of grass and leaves to sleep on. That was all. No bathroom, no separate rooms, no walls. The roof could shelter us from the rain, but nothing could bar the fog and dew that fell with darkness every night.

After the house was built, the Khmer Rouge gave us our assignments. First, we had to clear the trees and burn them to make room for the crops. Then we had to scatter the ashes that remained over the fields as a fertilizer. In this new world, it was the burden of the old, dead things to give life to the new things that would grow.

My father marched through the fresh earth, using a sharpened stick to punch a hole into it every few feet, and I would follow behind, laying three kernels of corn in each hole, and then gently tucking them in beneath a warm fold of dirt. We lived here two months, long enough to see them sprout, green and tender, and grow until they were almost as high as my waist, but we never got to see them mature. We were gone long before then.

Protected from the Wind

The people of Cambodia were divided, the Khmer Rouge said, into two groups. The "old people" and the "new". The old people had lived in the countryside all these years. They were the backbone of Cambodia, the true and loyal lifeblood of our people. The rural working class, these were the people who had born the burden of the country on their strong but weary shoulders. They were the ones who, unbeknownst to us, had looked on painfully at the luxury we, the urban middle class, had enjoyed all these years at their expense. We were the new people. A subtle invader, a parasite that had eaten the rice the old people had grown, feasted from the earth into which they had sweat. It was on their behalf that Cambodia had been reborn. The world had not been turned upside down, the Khmer Rouge told us. It had been finally turned right side up so that they were now the rulers, and we the vulnerable masses.

We did not know then the great movement and ideology behind this. We knew little of communism. Nor did we know the figure behind the ideas. It would be years before we first heard the name of the leader behind the Khmer Rouge. Born in 1925, Saloth Sar had grown up in my own city of Phnom Penh. It wasn't until he travelled to Paris on a scholarship that he became involved with the Communist Party. He returned to our city four years later with a radical plan for a right-side-up Cambodia. He worked as a teacher at a private school, but his real focus was on the dream he had for his country. That was when he took on his new name, Pol Pot. For the last twelve years, he had been living in the countryside, building support for his cause, amassing a great army for his Khmer Rouge, his Red Cambodia.

Protected from the Wind

But we didn't know any of this. We didn't know the mechanizations of the Khmer Rouge and how it worked. We didn't know who had engineered it or who oiled its gears. What we did know was that we needed to hide.

Behind the corn fields stretched a vast and thick forest. After we were finished with our duties for the day, my father took us back into the forest and showed us a tree whose branches hung with small black fruits like olives. We broke off several branches from this tree and dragged them back to the house. Back home, we dropped the whole thing, branch and all, into a pot of boiling water and stirred until it turned the water a murky black. Into this we plunged our clothes, scarves, bed sheets, everything that had color. Once they'd absorbed as much dye as they could hold, we laid them out to dry, only to do it all again the next day. Each item went through two or three rounds in the boiling dye. Pink, blue, green, it all melted away in this pot. The delicate flowers on my mother's blouse. The little sailboat print on my brother's shirt. The butterflies on Hong's. They all drowned in the black dye.

"We have to hide who we are," my father told us as we donned our newly gray clothing. "We have to blend in. We can't let them know we had money or nice things. If they ask, I was a jewelry shop laborer. I didn't own the business, you understand? And don't say anything about nice jewelry. No gold or rubies. We were no one. We are just like everyone else, you understand?"

And just like everyone else, we turned to the community for our food. The town leader distributed rice from his hut in the center of town. He was an "old comrade." It was with his people that we wanted to blend in. But even if we told them nothing of the jewelry store my father had owned or of the golden chains he could craft, they knew we were not one of them. They knew we were from the city.

We "new people" registered our families at his hut. Ours was a family of nine. So we were given nine cups of rice to last us the week. We carried them home and cooked it in our hut. But it was not enough. So my father took Chun, Kann, and me, and we went out into the forest to see what we could find. Sometimes we found fruit trees with long slender pods that, if they were *just* right, we could crack them open to find a row of plump seeds in a bed of sweet, juicy flesh. We would gather these up and carry them home so that my mother could cook the seeds with our rice and we could suck the rest of the fruit from its shell. Sometimes we would find mushrooms, big beautiful clusters of them. These, too, we would scoop up and bring them home where they would soon become a delicious soup to be poured on top of our rice.

The only happiness I ever felt, in those days in the valley, was when we found a new source of food. When our bags were full of something that would soon fill our bellies and our hunger would be gone – for a little while at least. It was all we thought about now. Hunger.

I still had my box tucked away in my leafy bed, but it wasn't important anymore. Besides, its supply was rapidly diminishing. My mother had taken most of my rubber bands to make those bags that we filled with our precious finds. She tied them around our scarves to make them a tube, a sack for carrying things. Once we found some fish, and she strapped them together with my rubber bands. And another time, when the wind was blowing, she took a whole rope of them to tie our bags of clothes down to keep them from blowing away. The first time she had asked, "Sida, may I use your rubber bands?" I had hesitated. They were mine. They had been my treasure. But before long, I didn't care. What were rubber bands in a world where there was so little food and no walls to keep the morning damp off our skin?

And my marbles? They were dumped into a bucket with our scarves and clothes. There was no soap for washing, but a good tumble in the water with my marbles could get most of the dirt off our smaller pieces.

It was ok. There was no time for play anymore. When we were done with work, we were so tired and so hungry, we didn't want to waste our effort on games or singing. We didn't even talk about the old times. We would only sit and wonder when we would next find food and whether it would be enough.

Our rice rations grew smaller and smaller. One week we were only given two cups for the whole family. The next week, we were only given one. And some weeks, we carried our bucket to the leader's hut only to be turned away. "We're out of rice," they would say. "Come back next week."

It was around that time that Chao got sick. He'd been my little shadow since we'd moved here. Too little to have any chores of his own, Chao would follow me as I did mine. But one day he didn't. I would look behind me, expecting him to be there watching like he always was, but he wasn't. He just stayed in the hut and slept. He was too tired to get up. Too tired to talk. Too tired even to smile. I remember lying down beside him, my face just inches away from his. I poked him. Just a gentle finger pressed into his cheek. I wanted him to say something. I wanted him to laugh. I wanted to see his dimple again. I wanted to know that he was still there, that he was still my Chao. I shook him a little by the shoulders. He opened his eyes, but they were empty. Their sparkle was gone.

While Chao was lying sick in his bed, the Khmer Rouge came back through our town. "If you want to move, pack up your stuff! Angka needs workers in another town." All around us were the sounds of packing. "This place is poison!" they were saying. "Epidemic!" I heard the word whispered in our neighbor's conversations. "Let's get out while we can."

But Chao was sick and couldn't travel. I hoped that the next place would be better. I hoped that we'd get more rice, that we wouldn't be so cold at night. But I also worried. I worried, as I watched family after family leave, that Chao wouldn't get well in time, that we would lose our chance to go. That we would be stuck here. I worried about these things as I watched my mother boil herbs in the pot, a remedy one of the other women had told her about and then hold it gently to his lips. I worried about it as I watched her wash the body of Chao – who didn't have the strength to go outside to the bathroom. She held him out in front her and gently ran a wet cloth over his small frame. That was all that it was – a frame. Tiny bones covered in a thin layer of skin. I could count his tiny ribs – ten, eleven, twelve- as she dribbled the water over them.

What I didn't know was that my mother had different worries. I didn't hear her whispered conversations with my father after the rest of us had gone to sleep. "If we leave now," she would say to him, "and he dies on the way, there will be no burial. We'll have to leave him on the side of the road." And her voice would choke on the words. I didn't know that we

Protected from the Wind

weren't waiting for Chao to get better. We were waiting for him to die.

I came home from my hunt in the forest one day to find him, not laying on his bed as usual, but wrapped in my mother's arms. She was shaking with tears, but he wasn't moving. Soon they were all crying. Hong, Chun, all of my siblings. We held onto one another and cried.

My father and Chun walked out to the hill behind our house and dug a grave on the base of hill. There his grave would be protected from the wind that might blow away the dirt and expose him. At least in death, Chao would be protected, a thing we couldn't give him in life.

We wrapped him a straw mat – he was so small, even in the mat, too small – and laid him in the grave. I didn't help with any of this. I just watched. I watched my little brother disappear beneath the earth. My mother said a prayer, and then, though her tears, she spoke to Chao. "I loved you, my son. I'm sorry, we have to leave you here. Stay here in peace, my son."

My father didn't say anything. He just stood there, looking at his son's grave.

We went back to the hut and packed our things. The next day, we boarded a wagon and left for a new home, our golden chain one link shorter.

Chapter 5

Angka's Children

From that point on, it seemed, the Khmer Rouge was intent on peeling us away from our family, our roots, our culture, and our community. One at a time, they took us, links plucked from a golden chain. But they didn't see it that way. They saw it as connecting us to something better instead: one giant chain that stretched the length of all of Cambodia. They called in Angka.

The community, the country, the people, the organization that ran it all, this was Angka. Angka was our real family, they said. Our mother, our father, our brothers and sisters, all rolled into one. And just like a mother or father, they said, it would take care of us. Angka knew what we needed and would meet our needs. And just like a good son or daughter, we must serve Angka.

First Angka came for my brother Chun. They called us to a meeting one evening. Every family in the town went. I remember them shouting out their orders, and then they read a list of names. Chun's name was among them. They called it their Number One Force – the young men, ages fourteen and up, full of strength and energy. "Tomorrow you will leave for your workplace!" they announced. "These are Angka's orders. Anyone who does not obey the orders of Angka will suffer consequences." When the women began to cry, the leaders chastised them. "Don't hold your children back. They belong to Angka! They are not your children anymore; they belong to Angka."

Angka's Children

At first, I didn't understand why my mother was crying as we walked home. I didn't understand why our neighbors came by our hut later that night asking in whispered voices if there was any way out, anywhere they could run, any place they could hide their sons. "But where would you go? There's nowhere to go!" was the only answer to these questions.

My mother packed a bag for Chun, wiping tears from her eyes as she did. I began to understand then that I was losing him, my bong.

"Bong Chun, you have to go?" I asked him.

He nodded, his face sad. The mirth, the mischievous twinkle, the crooked smile of the boy who had raced his bike on the roof, had long been gone.

"Don't go," I pleaded, holding his hand, as if I could hold the chain together with the strength of my fingers. "Don't go!"

Chun looked at me. "I have to go," he said. "If you disobey Angka, they will kill us. Maybe if one person doesn't go, they will kill the whole family."

In the morning he left for the meeting, but we followed him. There was no one to stop us and we wanted to hold onto him as long as we could.

The young men all gathered in front of the leader's house. Four Khmer Rouge soldiers called their names. When they saw that every boy was there, they led them away. We watched them walk down the road. We watched until we could see them no more.

My mother was crying as she watched. I held her hand. A leader who stood by scolded her. "Why are you crying?" he asked. "They are not your children! They are Angka's! Don't be sad anymore. From now on, everyone has to work for Angka, to do what Angka tells them to do. Go back home."

Angka's Children

It was only a few days later that they came for my sister. We were in our hut when we heard it. A fat lady, one of the Khmer Rouge leaders, was walking through the town screaming out, "Teenage girls!" At first, we thought we must have misheard her, but she called it out over and over. "Teenage girls! Come with us to the work place. Angka needs you."

Teenage girls? We wondered. *How could they want the girls?* In Cambodia we always kept our girls close to home, sheltered and protected. We didn't send them out from their homes alone. They couldn't possibly be asking this of us. But Angka didn't follow the old rules.

We tried to hide behind the house, but we couldn't escape them. Another leader came riding around on a bike, circling the huts. "Get to the meeting!" he shouted. "You have 30 minutes. These are Angka's orders."

So we ran back into the hut where my parents were frantic. Hong was crying as my mother packed her bag with shaking hands. My father helped my mother. I stood by and watched, tears slipping down my cheeks.

And then their eyes fell on me. I could tell by the look that came across their faces what they were thinking. "What happened? Are they going to take me, too?"

They didn't answer. They just looked at me, my mother's eyes red-rimmed and teary, my father's wide. At ten-years-old, I wasn't a "teenage girl," but if this Angka would call even girls from their families, there was nothing they wouldn't touch. Their eyes might fall on me, just as my parents' had, and they might think to themselves, "That girl there, she could work".

"What should I do?" I asked.

Angka's Children

My father took me by the shoulders. "Stay in the house. Don't show yourself. Maybe if they don't see you…"

So I said goodbye to Hong at the house. I held her close, my wet cheek against hers. "Goodbye, Bong Hong," I said, and she was gone. I didn't watch her go to the meeting. I didn't watch as she gathered with all the other girls whose names were called. I didn't watch as she marched off to the work camp for which Angka had chosen her. My mother stayed with me at the hut. Both of my bong were gone.

The next few months were quiet. There was no fun, no laughter, no singing. Nothing to look forward to. We worked all day. My job was to take care of the town garden, to water the tomatoes, yucca, yams, peanuts, and pumpkins. Thy and Kann came with me, pulling at the weeds around the crops. At night, we ate our small portions of rice. We never heard back from Chun or Hong. There was no way to know where they were, if they were safe, if we would ever see them again.

One day, Angka came again, and this time, they came for me. The leaders called for a meeting, everyone had to attend. At the meeting, they said that Angka needed the children, both girls and boys. They read off our names.

As we walked to our hut, my mother's head sagged like she was tired, tired of losing her children. With tired hands she packed my bag, just as she had my brother's and my sister's. This time, I knew, there was no hiding. I had to go.

That night, as I lay down on my mat, she spread her warm palm against my back. "If you are ever in trouble, Sida," she whispered. "Pray to God. He will help you." Because for the first time, she would not be there to help me herself. "Pray to God," she whispered again. But when she said it, I thought of the big stone Buddha in the temple in Phnom Penh. I thought of bowing down on the steps before it and waiting while my parents finished their prayers. I thought of the incense that Hong used to light and the way it would rise into the air and then disappear. I didn't want to pray to God. When I had trouble, I wanted to turn to my parents.

In the morning, I took my bag and I stood up to go. My father knelt down so that he could look me in the eye. "Sida, you must blend in," he said. "Don't make yourself a leader. Don't speak out. Don't stand out. You need to be calm. You need to hide your identity. Don't do anything to draw attention to yourself. Do you understand what I'm saying?"

I nodded.

"Go and maybe they will let you come back soon."

I went with my father's words fresh in my mind. I met with all the other children in front of the leader's house. Together we all walked away. This time I was the golden link, bent open and slipping off the chain.

It was about a six-hour walk to our new assignment. By the time we arrived it was nearly evening. They pointed us to a long rectangular hut where we would stay, and we set up our bed mats side by side in a row, boys on one side, girls on the other, feet to feet. Then they served us our dinner. A real bowl-full of rice, much more than the few grains we would get back in town. We ate it hungrily and went to sleep.

In the morning when the sun rose, they woke us with the shriek of a whistle. It was time to go to work. I was given an empty basket and sent to a giant, dusty hole where the Mei Kong - the camp leaders - were digging with shovels. It was my job to fill the basket with dirt and carry it across to the mound that they were building about fifty feet away. Back and forth I carried my basket, and beside me, sixty other children were doing the same. It was a while before I realized what we were doing. On the one side, we were digging irrigation to allow water to flow to the rice fields. On the other, we were building a road, a high one that would stand above the floods during monsoon season. All around us hundreds of people were working, men, women, children. Who knows, maybe my brother or sister was there, not far from me, working, but I had no way of finding out, no way of looking for them.

At the end of each day, we dragged ourselves back to our huts, ate our rice, rinsed the dirt off our legs and arms, and got ready for bed. But before we could sink into the sleep we longed for, the Mei Kong stepped into our hut and screamed the dreaded word, "Meeting! Meeting!" So we trudged our way outside to the bonfire, where they taught us about communism. "The children belong to Angka!" they told us. "Angka is moving us forward! We are the generation to make this country grow!" And then we sang a song "Victory, victory to communism!" At last, we walked back to our huts. I curled up under the quilt my mother had made me –now a dull patchwork of brown and gray—and fell asleep. All too soon, I was woken again by the sound of the whistle and the thud of the Mei Kong's feet kicking mine. "Get up! Go to work!"

I worked every day at the camp for a few months, but at last the road and the ditch were finished. It was just in time, because the monsoon rains had come. "Go home!" Mei Kong told us with a wave of her hands. And with that, we packed up our bags and left. I didn't know exactly where home was, but I followed the crowds, knowing that many of the other children had come from the same town as me.

    We were about halfway there when it started raining. It began as a gentle drizzle but grew into a feverish rain with thick, heavy drops. I had a little plastic sheet in my bag for occasions like this, and I held it over my head as long as I could, but my arms grew tired, and after a while, it became clear that no plastic would keep me dry in this deluge. The land around me began to look familiar, and I knew that I was close, but not as close as I would have liked. By the time I reached the town, it was nearly dark –just a hint of a vanished sun on the horizon—and my hair and clothes were heavy with rainwater. I don't know how I found my way back to the hut because I was so tired, too tired to even realize what I was doing or where I was. I don't remember the faces of my mother and father in our doorway. I don't remember their relief in seeing me, their kisses on my face, or their warm hands on my cold ones. I don't remember them helping me inside, changing me out of my wet clothes, and lying me down in my bed. I don't remember falling asleep.

Chapter 6

Where the Water Kept on Flowing

When morning came, I didn't get up. I don't know how long I slept, but when I woke, my body ached and trembled with cold. My mother stood nearby, boiling a pot of water with herbs that smelled like the last few days with Chao. They wafted, steamy, through the hut. And then I sank back into sleep. I woke again to the touch of a cold spoon against my lips, followed by a splash of bitter liquid into my mouth. I twisted away at the taste, but my mother pressed another spoonful to my mouth and another until I closed my lips tight and wouldn't drink anymore. And then I slipped back down into unconsciousness where I could not feel the tender misery of my muscles or the chills that crept across them. But too soon, someone was lifting me up out of rest again, my father propping my body against his own. My mother was there, too, with her spoon. This time she had added some palm sugar to the water, but it still tasted awful. I tried to swallow it, one sip after another, but then my stomach began to churn, and before I knew it, it was spilling back out of my mouth and onto my quilt. I fell asleep to the gentle motions of my mother's hands wiping me clean of my vomit.

In my sleep, the ache was gone, as were the bitter herbs. Instead, I was playing badminton in the street in front of our apartment building. I had to swing hard to fling the birdie into the blue sky, and when it came back,

Where the Water Kept on Flowing

it always came fast. I had to run to get there in time, but I always made it, just managing to swat the birdie with my racket and send it back into the blue. At last, I was tired, glowing from the delicious exercise. I sat down to eat some candy. There were whole handfuls of it, the kind that Chun used to give me in exchange for his compass when I'd held it hostage. I unwrapped the first piece. I was lifting it to my mouth, when suddenly the candy was shaken from me. It was falling away, and instead I saw my father's face, leaning in close to mine, his hand slapping my cheek over and over again. The aches of my body came rushing back. "Who am I?" He asked, leaning even closer. "Who am I?"

I had to force my mouth to make the motions. "Pa," I said.

"Okay. Go back to sleep." He let go of me then, and I slipped back down, down, to where I could feel no more. This time I was riding my bicycle on the roof of our apartment building. The wind was racing across my skin, and I was racing across it, and the sky above me stretched forever and ever, and I was free. Then I stopped the bike in front of a large pound cake, yellow and spongey. I cut myself a slice and was just lifting it to my lips, when he shook me, the cake dissolving into oblivion. His face was there again, leaning in towards mine. "Who am I?"

"Pa!" I moaned. "Can't you let me eat first, before you wake me up?"

I heard laughter bubbling in the background, and then I sank back down into sleep. I slept like this, for what I think turned out to be about a month. I woke only for my father's interrogations to ensure that I had not slipped into something deeper than sleep and for my mother's spoonfuls of bitter herbs. Sometimes, she tried

Where the Water Kept on Flowing

to feed me rice soup, the kind they give to babies, but even that I couldn't manage to swallow. In all that time, I never got up to go to the bathroom, so she must have cleaned me as she had cleaned Chao. I slept through that. I slept through everything. In my sleep, I was always playing, like I was the little girl I used to be. And in my sleep, there was always food, delicious and tantalizing.

But while I slept, my body slowly slipped away from me. First my feet and then my legs all the way up to my hips. Each time I woke, I found that I couldn't move them. They lay like foreign things attached to my body.

In was during this time that the Khmer Rouge came through and ordered us to move. They demanded that we make our way to the railroad tracks a few miles away, where a train would take us to our new assignment. So while I slept, my parents packed. We had too many things, things we could not live without, more than we could carry, so my family decided to carry it in two trips. My mother and my siblings would carry as much as they could for a few hundred feet. Then they would stop and, leaving my mother and Peou there, the rest would come back to where my father waited with the second load. These they would all carry to my mother, and then they would begin the process again. In this way we would inch down the road to the railway.

After all the bags had been packed, my mother and her able-bodied children had left with their first load. When Thy and Kann could be seen heading back, my father crouched down in front of me. He pulled me up against his back, wrapped his scarf around both my body and his, and tied it in a tight knot at his chest. He stood up, and for the first time in a month, my body was lifted from my bed. As my brother and sister carried their second load, my father carried me, my feet dragging, useless, on the dirt behind him.

The road was a raised dirt mound, just like the one I had helped to build a month before, and it stretched straight before us, a thick brown line leading directly to the railroad. It was crowded. Beside us, hundreds of people walked, carrying all of their belongings with them. They must have been evacuating the entire town to new assignments.

As he walked, I noticed that there was something about my father's body that was strange. He arms were bigger than I remembered. They were swollen and puffy. In my curiosity, I pressed my finger into one of them. I watched his skin sink under the weight of my finger, and when I pulled away, the little dent I had made remained for a long moment. I was puzzled by this unusual malleability.

My father must have carried me for a half a mile before he grew too tired to continue and sat down by the side of the road to rest. He untied the scarf, and I dropped to the ground. My father sat next to me. When he was ready again, he tied me onto his back again and we resumed. We carried on this way for a long time, walking, and then resting. Sometimes as we walked, I would see my mother and the others as they walked past or as they sat guarding our belongings. They were brief glimpses, and then they were gone.

My father stropped then, for a break it seemed, just like all the others. He set me on the ground, his breath heavy and wheezing. "Sida, I cannot carry you anymore." He took several more breaths before he spoke again. "Look at me, I'm all swollen." He pointed to his feet which were as bloated as his arms. As an experiment, I poked one of them, and just like his arm, the impression of my finger lingered.

When he had caught his breath, my father stood up again. He left me on the road and walked down in the bushes that grew along its side. I lay there in the dirt, waiting, while a steady parade of feet passed by me. I thought nothing of this, figuring he was looking for help, or maybe going to the bathroom. Never did it occur to me that he really meant what he had just said. When my father returned, he was carrying a thick stick in his hand. "Sida, I cannot carry you anymore," he said, and there was a firmness in his voice. "You're going to walk."

I looked at him for a moment, unable to understand. *But I can't walk,* I thought. *I can't even stand.*

"Look at me, Sida," he said. I looked at his body. It was thin, and yet somehow seemed artificially inflated, his chest bloated with the breath he was still trying to catch. "I'm all swollen. I have no energy." My father held the stick out to me. "Stand up," he said.

But of course, I didn't. I couldn't. There was nothing I could do.

He reached down and lifted me by my armpits. He put the stick in my hand and set it firmly in the ground. Slowly he let go of my armpits. Immediately I sank. His hands caught me and lifted me back up. "Stand up," he said. Again, I tried, and again I fell. "Stand up. Stand up." He said it over and over, each time lifting me back up and clasping my hands around the top of the stick.

But then finally it happened. He slipped his fingers from beneath my arms, and yet I stayed upright. I clung to the stick with a tenacious grip, and my arms were trembling with the weight, but I was standing. It

Where the Water Kept on Flowing

only lasted a few seconds, and then I couldn't do it anymore. I dropped, and my father caught me. "Stand up," he said again and put the stick back into my hands. I held on longer this time. My body began to sink up and down the stick with the wavering strength of my arms, but I stayed upright.

"Ok, walk," my father said.

But I couldn't. My legs wouldn't obey me. They weren't a part of me anymore.

He said it again. "Walk."

So I tried. I pushed one foot forward. At the shift in weight, the other leg collapsed beneath me and I fell. My father caught me and lifted me back up.

"Walk." He propped me back against the stick and let go of my arms. "Walk, or I will have to leave you." The voice in which he said this was as stiff and brittle as the stick in my hands.

I began to cry.

"Walk!"

I couldn't bear the thought of him leaving, of me all alone. A single link in a chain is nothing by itself. So easily lost. So easily swept away with dust.

"If you don't walk, I will have to leave you here."

"No, no, no!" I cried. "Don't leave me here, Pa! Don't leave me!"

"Then walk!" He said it one last time. "Walk!" And then he left me. He walked forward down the road, and I was alone.

I had heard of people who died this way. They got sick or injured and their families left them behind. There was nothing left for them to do but to die there alone. I didn't want to die alone. So I tried to walk.

I pushed one foot forward. The other leg stayed. I was still standing. I took a deep breath and tried it again

Where the Water Kept on Flowing

with the other foot. It moved forward, and I was still standing. I shuffled forward a few feet before my legs buckled and I fell. This time my father was not there to catch me.

I lay crumpled in the road with nothing but my stick, my ragged breath, my trembling legs, and the sticky tears on my face. *What can I do?* I asked myself. *I can't get up by myself. There's nothing I can do.* I began to wonder. *Will I die here?*

But I didn't want to die alone. Passing by me, feet were still slowly plodding along heavily. One after another, people and all their belongings moved past me. They were all heading to the railroad. "Excuse me," I called to the next pair of feet that passed by. "Please, could you please help me up?"

It was a young woman, not much older than Hong. She stopped, dropped the bag of rice she was carrying onto the road, and leaned down. She lifted me just as my father had, and I pressed the stick firmly into the ground. "Thank you," I said, and she picked her bag back up and moved on.

So I tried it again. One foot forward. Then the other. A few more steps until I collapsed again. I lay there breathing, trying to capture as much air in my lungs as I could. And then I called out to the next traveler on the road, a man struggling under the weight of a giant pot. "Excuse me, sir. Could you please lift me up?"

This was how I moved down the road, a few feet at a time, huffing and puffing, lifted periodically by the kindness of strangers. It was slow, and it was painful, but I was moving. I would eventually make it.

That was what I thought until I came to the ditch. I had helped build a road just like this one at the children's work camp, so I knew what it was. The road

Where the Water Kept on Flowing

was a raised mound, lifted above the mud and water of the rainy season, but every few hundred feet, it was interrupted by a ditch to allow the irrigated water to flow through. These were not shallow indentations in the road, but deep ruts. This one was about ten feet deep, a steep slope down to the water that ran in a muddy stream to the other side of the road. On the other side of this 5-foot-wide stream, another steep slope ran ten feet back up to where the road resumed.

When I reached the ditch, I sank to the ground beside it. There was no way I could cross. Even if I managed to make it down that slope, which was surely impossible, I couldn't cross the water without drowning. Its current was slow but steady. It would sweep me away into the irrigation channel on the side of the road. And even if, by some miracle, I made it across the stream alive, how would I ever climb the ten-foot slope up to the next stretch of road?

I sat by the edge of the ditch, and I watched the water slink by. It moved steadily, its pace constant. Beside me, travelers were climbing down into the ditch, wading through the water which reached up to their chests, and then climbing up the slope to continue on dry road. One by one they went by me, moving at their steady pace. An old woman that I had seen before walked by me. She stared at me with pity in her eyes as she climbed down into the water and crossed, but she didn't stop. She kept moving. And around the bodies of all these people with their bags slung over their shoulders, the water flowed. It kept flowing.

What am I going to do? I thought. I looked through the crowd for someone I knew. *Where are my mother and Peou? Kann? Thy?* It had been a long time since I'd seen them. They must have gotten way ahead.

Where the Water Kept on Flowing

A cold feeling swept through me, and my body began to tremble. *Am I going to die? Am I going to die here, alone?*

But then, on the other side of the stream, I saw something I hadn't seen in a long time. It was the tall slender shape of my brother, my bong. It was Chun. He was walking towards me. He splashed through the stream and up the slope to me. Then, reaching down, he swung me onto his back.

"Where have you been?" I cried, feeling tears rising up again at this unexpected salvation. "Where is everyone?" He didn't answer me but began carefully to descend the slope towards the water. I wrapped my arms around his neck, just like I had on all those bike rides on the roof, when we were flying as fast as Chun's feet could pedal, but there was no laughing, no teasing now. Back then, we had played at fear. Now we knew that fear was not a game. As he stepped into the water, I tightened my grip around his neck. I watched the water moving, and I imagined myself moving with it away, away from Chun, down into the irrigation channels. I clung to him with all my might.

He swatted at my arms with his hand. "Loosen up, Sida! Loosen up!" I did my best to loosen them, but the water was still flowing around us fast, and my fear was still rippling along with it.

At last we emerged from the water, and he climbed up the slope and onto the road. There, Chun set me on my feet and handed me the stick. "Don't cross the water," he told me. "When you get to the water again, wait for me." And with that, he walked away.

I began to hobble forward as I had before. But this time it was different. This time I knew my brother would come back for me. This time I knew I wasn't

Where the Water Kept on Flowing

really alone. This time, I knew I would reach the railway.

It was a long walk, shuffling forward bit by bit until I fell, waiting for a stranger to lift me back to my feet and, shuffling some more, but eventually I made it to the next ditch. So, I did as Chun said. I sat down and waited.

It wasn't too long before he came for me. This time, he had a blanket slung across his back. He knelt down, and I climbed on, but I was nervous. The blanket was smooth and slid easily between my brother's skin and me. "Why did you put this on?" I asked. "I'm slipping."

He didn't say anything but carried me down the slope and into the stream. I clung to him with my arms around his neck and my knees pressed to his sides, but still the blanket slid around between us. Again, I could see myself in the water. Slipping, slipping away. But I managed to stay on his back all the way across the stream and up to the next road. Then, as he set me down with my stick, he slid the blanket off of his bare back and pointed to his back bone. "Look at my bones, Sida." He said. Chun had always been slender, but he was even thinner now. His back bone rose visible beneath his skin, and next to it, each of his ribs reached around his body. Then he pointed to me. "Your bones rub against my bones, and it hurts." I knew that after my illness, my bones stuck out even more than his. There was nothing around them but a thin sheet of skin.

He left me then and walked on forward, and I followed with my stick and my slow shuffling.

We did this probably six or seven more times. I would slowly make my way to the next ditch where I would wait. And each time, Chun came for me, and carried me across, and left me to keep moving slowly. Each time, I seemed to get a little stronger. The journey took us the whole day. The sun rose till it was high in the sky. Then it began to slowly sink towards the ground, and the farther is sank, the less I leaned on my stick, until I found, at last, that I was able to walk without the stick at all. So by myself, on my own two legs, I walked in the dimming light until I came to a place where the crowds were thick. They were sitting now, rather than walking, many of them gathered around campfires. I knew this must be where we would wait for the train. I looked through the crowds for my family.

The first one I saw was my father. He, too, was walking through the crowds, looking. When he saw me, he beckoned me toward him. I followed him until I could see the rest of our family. I saw Chun, leaning over the campfire. Then I saw Kann, who jumped up, pointing a delighted finger at me. "Oh! Look who's here!" He sprang towards me. "Yay!" he cheered as he wrapped his little arms around me. Holding my hand, he led me to the rest of the campfire.

My mother looked up at me and smiled, holding out one inviting arm. I sat next to her, and she pulled me close. "Sida," she said with a smile. "Look at you. So dirty!" She took a damp cloth and washed my face.

Hong was there, stirring a pot of rice over the fire. Thy, Kann, and Chun were behind her arguing. "I'm going!" Kann was saying.

"No, you're too slow!" Chun told him.

"I'm fast!" Thy popped in.

"Where are you going?" I asked.

Thy pointed across the railroad tracks to a thick grove of trees. "To get some oranges!" There was a

Where the Water Kept on Flowing

sparkle in her eye, the kind we only saw at the prospect of a good food hunt.

I looked around at the crowds that spilled around the train tracks. There were no Khmer Rouge soldiers to be seen. No Mei Kong. It was our chance. Who knew how long it would last?

I turned to my dad. "Can I go?"

"No," he said, firmly.

In the end, it was Chun and my father who went. They and a whole crowd of people from other families made their dash across the tracks in one thick group; then they disappeared into the trees. The sun was sinking fast, and we watched as darkness spread across the tops of the trees. We waited, wondering if they had been caught, stealing from Angka.

But after twenty minutes, we saw them running, my father, my brother, and all of the others. Each was carrying a giant bag full of oranges.

As soon as they arrived, my mother cut the oranges into wedges, each one bright and moist and dripping with promise. I thrust one up to my lips and sucked all the sweet juice out of it. It was the first piece of food I remembered having since I had fallen sick. I slurped three oranges this way, one wedge after another, until I was full.

Night was upon us now, and the campfire shrank to a faint glow. I leaned back on the ground, my whole family around me. All my brothers and sisters, even my bong lay nearby. I could hear their breathing, forming a blanket of air around us.

The sky was full of stars. The breeze was dancing across my face, and my stomach was plump with orange juice. There was nothing between me and those beautiful lights in the sky. No roof. No aches. No hunger.

Chapter 7

Why Are You Still Alive?

We waited at the railroad tracks for three days. They were good days, as good as days got under the Khmer Rouge. Each morning, I woke up to oranges. I ate until I was full, and then I rested. When I was ready, I ate some more. There was no hunger during those three days. Only the delicious, sticky, dribble down my chin and fingers. I may have eaten other food while we waited, probably some rice or some soup, but all I remember are the oranges.

On the second day, a familiar face suddenly appeared. It was my uncle, my father's youngest brother. My father's face lit up when he saw him. He pulled his little brother to himself so that their heads touched. "Where have you been?" he asked, though the answer didn't really matter. Chun was the next to greet him. My uncle was only a few years older than Chun, and they had been close friends back in Phnom Penh, often heading out into the city to do see a movie or play ping pong together. I hadn't seen him since those days. Now he was here with us in this very different world.

He was as happy as we were to have found one another. "I'll just run back to the town to grab my things!" he said with a wide smile. "I'll be back in a couple of hours." And off he went.

The mood was as happy as the oranges on which we chewed that afternoon. Our chain, it seemed, would grow by one link. But as the hours slipped by into night, the mood soured. When we woke in the morning, and our uncle was still not there, the cheerfulness was gone. But still we waited. Still we hoped.

We waited and hoped until the train came. Then we had to climb aboard without my uncle.

"He must have gotten stopped," my father said. "They probably sent him off somewhere else." Sorrow made his voice sag. He was wondering if he would ever see his little brother again. And he wouldn't. That was the last time we saw my uncle.

This was where the wondering began. We would always wonder what had happened. Always marvel at how we had been so close, so close to clasping our hands together in a chain. And the wondering lasted for years. Slowly it withered into knowing, but only half-knowing. Knowing that he must be dead, but never when or how, and what we knew, we knew only because we never heard from him again.

The train took us to the rice farms. After we had selected our spot and built a small hut, we began irrigating the fields and planting the seeds. We were working together as a family again, and it was my job, along with the younger kids, to thin the young plants in the rice fields. When the grain flourished and grew so that the ground was tight and the space insufficient, we pulled the rice shoots, tied them into green bundles, and planted them in new fields where there would be room.

One day, my father called us in from the rice fields. We all gathered in the hut. There was a smile on his face and a bounce in his step as he ushered us all in. We hadn't seen him this excited since Phnom Penh. "We're moving!" he said. And the way he said it, I knew he didn't mean to just another rice farm, another assignment for Angka. "We're going to Vietnam."

Why Are You Still Alive?

I didn't know much about Vietnam, but I could tell by my father's face and the way he said the word that it must be wonderful. Or at least it must have been different from here. Really, wonderful and different-from-here were the same thing.

"But we have to pretend to be Vietnamese," he said. Apparently, the Khmer Rouge had announced that, wanting to save Cambodia for the true Cambodians, anyone who could prove he was Vietnamese would be granted transportation across the border to his homeland of Vietnam. My father saw this as our way out. "We have to learn the language," my father told us. "There's going to be a test."

This became our new task, learning the Vietnamese words that we expected to be on the test. I had to learn *Den an yay?* which means *What is your name?* And I had to be prepared to answer the question *Moy mei douy?* or *How old are you?*" Then we all learned the numbers 1-100. We repeated them to one another as we worked in the rice field. We said them over and over as we carried the tender rice shoots from the old field in which they had been born to the new field, one where there was room for them to grow, for them to thrive. We practiced them as we cooked our rice in the hut, and as we scrubbed the pot clean afterwards.

We were practicing them, my father and I, as we walked through the woods gathering firewood, when we heard a loud gasp. "That's the girl! That's the one!" exclaimed a voice. It was an old woman, walking with her family nearby. Her face was familiar, but I didn't know her name. She pointed a bony finger at me. "I can't believe it! You should have been dead long ago!" She turned back to her family. "I saw her on the side of road, completely lame." She stepped closer and peered

Why Are You Still Alive?

at me with narrow eyes, the way you would peer at a mango to decipher whether or not it had rotted yet. "Why are you still alive?"

I wanted to tell her that not only was I alive, but I was going to keep on living! I wanted to tell her that we were going to Vietnam, that things were going to get much better for me. I wanted to tell her that it was very rude to tell someone you couldn't believe they weren't dead. But she was an old woman, and I was merely a child, so I had to be quiet. Even when she was gone, I said nothing of her rudeness or of the surge of anger it had sparked in me. And my father said nothing of it to me. Instead, we resumed our practice of the Vietnamese numbers. Because we were determined to survive. And we were convinced that this was how we would do it.

On the day of our scheduled test, we walked into town full of hope. There were several long lines in front of a Khmer Rouge warehouse. They stretched far out in the sun. But it was no matter; we didn't mind waiting for the prospect of a new life. So we sat and waited, all eight of us. Finally, it was our turn, and they called us in for our test.

I never got the chance to show off what I'd learned, to proudly answer the question "Moy mei douy?" with my age "Moy mok." They didn't speak to us children at all. Instead, they asked my mother and father all the questions. The Khmer Rouge said a few things in Vietnamese, and then they pointed to the door. "Go back," they said.

We all walked outside. I wasn't sure what had happened. *Are we going back to the hut to pack?* I wondered. *Are we going to Vietnam?* But when I looked to my father to ask these questions, I knew the answer.

Why Are You Still Alive?

His body drooped as if he were suddenly very tired, and his smile was gone. "We didn't pass," he said quietly.

But there were still all these lines outside the warehouse. There were still all these other people who had hope. And we wanted so badly to go to Vietnam. We wanted so badly to get away. So we joined at the end of another line. *Maybe they'll let us take the test again,* I thought. But the sun rose high in the sky and then began to sink. And the lines moved slowly. Finally, my father said, "Come on. We're not going to get in."

We walked home in disappointment.

Some of our neighbors had passed the test. They packed their bags with smiles on their faces. "We're going to Vietnam!" they said. We hugged them goodbye and tried to be happy for them, but we couldn't shake the sadness, because we were not going, we had to stay here. We watched them get on a boat. They had the same smile on their face, the same bounce in their step, that my father had had that day he called us into the hut. And they sailed off.

I didn't find out until years later that the Khmer Rouge were lying. Yes, they had sought to purge the Vietnamese and other foreigners from the population, but they had never had any intention of sending the Vietnamese home. Not one of those who had left for Vietnam ever made contact to report that they had arrived safely. They say that as soon as those boats made it to the ocean, the Khmer Rouge threw the passengers overboard.

What we had thought was our hope, what we had wanted so desperately, would have led to our deaths. But against our will, we had been spared. Against our will, we had survived.

Chapter 8

In Exchange for This

Monsoon season came, and with it, gloomy clouds, relentless rains, and the wet, damp feeling of hopelessness, the feeling that it would be this way forever.

I was sitting in the hut one day, surrounded by the dimness of the season, when I was suddenly seized by a cramp. But "cramp" seems far too innocuous a word for what was happening inside my body. It was more of a violent twisting, as though my internal organs were a sponge to be wrung out by strong hands. *I have to go to the bathroom*, I thought with urgency, and I ran out of the hut.

We didn't really have bathrooms, of course. We had the woods. I stopped at the first spot I could find, dug a hasty hole, and squatted over it to empty my bowels. I covered my hole and went back to the hut, but after a few minutes had passed, it was happening again.

This time, when I ran back out, I dug a deeper hole – I was confident there would be even more to fill it. But when I squatted, nothing happened. My body heaved and strained, it produced nothing. Well, almost nothing. There were a couple of drops, but they were bloody. I knew this was a bad sign. Bloody stool could be deadly. It could mean your intestines had ruptured.

This went on for several days, at least two weeks. My family went on with their regular work in the rice fields, but I stayed home with my cramps. My mother fed me some herbs that she hoped would help, but they did nothing. When I was in the hut, I sat in a ball hugging my knees to my stomach as if to hold in the pain, but it was not long before I was running again. I ran to the woods several times an hour all day and night, but every time, it was only a few drops, and what little there was always frightening. If it wasn't bloody, it was covered with a slippery mucus, or it was watery – as though the monsoon floods had somehow infiltrated my body.

Looking back, I suspect that what I suffered from was dysentery. What I remember most of that time was the pain. I have since felt many other kinds of pain. I have given birth to three children and yet, as I remember it, the agonies of childbirth are nothing to the pain of those cramps. I remember sitting in the corner of the hut, my sickness gripping me, crumpling me like paper from the inside out, and I remember thinking that I wanted it to go away. Even then, as an eleven-year-old girl, I compared what I was feeling to other kinds of pain I had endured before. I remembered these others with a kind of nostalgia: a splinter in my finger, a scraped knee, a toothache. I held each one in my mind and compared my current suffering to it.

That was when I first began to bargain. I wasn't sure who I was bargaining with. I'm not even sure I believed there was anyone out there to hear my negotiations. I only knew that there was nothing I could do to end this pain. And I knew that there was no person who could help me. So I hoped, rather than believed, that there was someone, something out there that could. Something or someone who could hear me. *A toothache,* I thought. *I'd take a toothache in exchange for this.* I imagined a toothache, even a bad one, and its blissful simplicity, the smallness of its location, its endurability, the fear of death that it did not bring. I worked my way

In Exchange for This

through each kind of pain I could imagine, offering it up as a trade.

My bargaining did not appear to work. The cramps did not swap themselves for another, milder malady. They did, however, begin to fade, and after a while they were gone all together. I wasn't sure what had caused them, and I was even less sure how I had survived, but here I was, a surprise again in the land of the living.

Chapter 9

To Keep the Light from Slipping Out

It was shortly after I recovered from dysentery that the Khmer Rouge moved us again. It had been a full two years now, since we had left our apartment in Phnom Penh. Two years that we'd followed the orders of Angka, going wherever it sent. This time, they planted us in Steang Chas, a river town that was surrounded by fields of corn. It was rainy season when we arrived, and the town was swaddled in a thick blanket of moisture. Moisture hung in the air, clung to our skin, weighed down our breath. Moisture gathered into a thick veil in the sky, forbidding the brilliance of sunlight to slip through. Every morning when we woke up, it was there, a shiny coat on the ground, an invisible haze in the air. There was no escaping it.

As with the other towns, we built our own home. It was my job to dig the holes for the posts while my mom took some of my younger siblings into the woods to gather palm leaves and branches. I dug for what seemed like forever, and when it was a foot deep, I stopped. Then my father came over and said, "Sida, you need to dig more. Otherwise, when the wind blows, the house will fall over." So we dug and dug until it was twice as deep. At last when it was done, we went to the next corner of the house to do it all over again. We started at the bottom and built up. My father and Chun laid bamboo beams across the top of the house while the

To Keep the Light from Slipping Out

rest of us wove the leaves together with vines and palm fibers. When they were ready, my father had to lift me onto his shoulders so that I could reach the top. Layer by layer, I tied the woven leaves to the beams. Layer after layer, we spread them over the top of the house to shield it from the rain.

It was under that roof that our family made the most permanent home we had during the Khmer Rouge years. This roof was important. We didn't realize, as we wove it together, that it was under this roof that irreversible events would transpire, the ones that would define our family story, the ones that would transform me from a girl into a woman. It was beneath these fronds that I would cry the most tears. It was here that I would do the most terrible thing, the thing I would regret my entire life. It was here that my life would change most.

It started with a small change. Instead of leaving us to cook our ration of food at home in our own hut and eat it as a family, here Angka not only distributed but prepared and served our food in a communal kitchen. At this kitchen, we all were given our portion of rice, and at the kitchen we ate it as a community. The community was, the Khmer Rouge frequently reminded us, our true family.

And yet that "true family" never did provide enough. We ate there twice a day, and we were served sometimes a cup of rice and sometimes only a few spoonfuls. Sometimes we were delighted to receive a whole bowl of something white and hot, scooped from the pot, but when it turned out to be rice porridge – rice thinned into a watery soup, we were always disappointed. When we were given rice porridge, I always saved the best for last, sipping at the water first, draining the bowl of its emptiness so that I could get the

To Keep the Light from Slipping Out

real food: the rice that settled at the bottom. Sometimes, when I had slurped the water, all that remained on the bottom were two teaspoons of soggy rice. Two teaspoons of rice for my meal. Two teaspoons that were trying so hard to be more. Two teaspoons spreading themselves into a big bowl of soup. But they were not enough.

So we had to supplement.

Sometimes we stole from the communal kitchen. I did this a couple of times, creeping in unnoticed when the room was either empty or too busy for anyone to notice. But Kann, he was the real master thief. He was quiet and small and could slip in and out of a room as smoothly as a gecko, without anyone noticing he'd ever been there. He'd go to the mill hut when the work day was over, and the adults assigned to milling would crowd in. The women would be gathered around the mill stone. The air would be bubbling with chatter punctuated with the occasional bark from a Mei Kong, and under all the noise, Kann would slide. No one would see him enter, and they wouldn't see his hand slipping one silent grain after another from the edge of the millstone into the hem of his shirt. They wouldn't see him leave, walking casually to our hut, where he would whisper a word to my mother. She would dig a quick hole in the ground for him to dump the rice in and then slide a bucket over the top so that no one could see it. We would mill the rice later at night. With no stone or pestle, we used our own hands and a thin cloth to break the husk from the grain.

Sometimes Kann would steal us processed rice from the communal kitchen, which was even better. He would sit near the rice pot, amid the hustle and bustle of the kitchen. He would slump on the bench and cast his gaze downward, looking bored, but all the while he was

To Keep the Light from Slipping Out

watching. Whenever a grain of rice slipped from the baskets onto the ground, he would notice. He waited for the moment when no one was looking and then swept it into his pocket. This was how he stole from Angka. One grain at a time. Each one as small and unnoticed as he was. And when he came home with a pocket full of rice, we were quiet, too. We didn't cheer or thank him. We didn't even smile. We took the treasure from his hand like it was nothing, buried it in the earth until it was safe to cook it. When night fell, my mother would cook the rice as quietly as Kann had stolen it. Then she would serve each of us, a spoonful a piece. It was a relief. It was a treat. Kann's gift. But it wasn't enough. We needed more.

Hong and Chun had been sent off to work camps again, and my parents spent their days working in Angka's fields here in Steang Chas. Peou joined them, her arm wrapped gently around my mother's thigh wherever she went, but Thy, Kann, and I were free during the day. We went out with the other children of the town, eager to find something, anything we could put in our mouths. Mostly we looked to the forest. As before, we found mushrooms. We gathered up any that we saw into our scarves and brought them home to be cooked and eaten. We didn't know the difference between a poisonous mushroom and a safe one, so in retrospect, I see that it was very fortunate that all the mushrooms we came across happened to be edible ones.

I can't say the same for all the foods we found in the forest. One day, we came upon a tree so heavily laden with seedpods, that we jumped and clapped our hands with delight. We gathered as many as we could and came into the town with bags stuffed full of the seeds, but we were stopped by an old woman. "You're

To Keep the Light from Slipping Out

not going to eat those, are you?" she asked, pointing to our bags.

It seemed like a ridiculous question. *Of course, we are! Who in their right mind wouldn't eat a feast like this?*

"You know they're poisonous," she said.

I didn't want to believe it was true. We had been so excited. So happy. And now this old woman was threatening that happiness.

"The tree where you found them, there were lots of them there?"

I nodded slowly, unsure why she was asking.

"Well, that tells you then," she said as if it were a matter of fact. "Why else do you think they'd all still be there? If they were edible, don't you think the birds would eat them? The monkeys? Don't you think someone else would have found them by now?"

I let my bag of pods sink to the ground as I thought about this. It was true. Big crops of food like this were unheard of. Where there was good food, it was always picked as soon as it was ripe.

"That's how you know," the old woman said.

So we returned home empty-handed that day, our hearts as heavy as our bags had been, sagging with the weight of deflated hopes.

Yes, whenever we found food, there was a good chance someone else had found it, too. Once, we came across a beautiful mango tree, lush with ripe mangos on its highest branches. I knew the danger. I knew that the mangos were not alone in that tree. But I also knew that their juice would be sweet, that their tender flesh would fill my stomach; I knew that they would ease my hunger. So I did it. I climbed the tree.

To Keep the Light from Slipping Out

As I climbed, I began to feel them. Crawling onto my fingers. Across my neck and onto my scalp. From the balls of my feet to my toes. I didn't swat at them or try to shake them off. That would only make room for new ones. Instead, I gritted my teeth and kept climbing.

The ants we have in Cambodia are the kind that bite with a sharp piercing grip that punctures the skin. To say that it is painful is an understatement. But I had to get to the mangos. I kept climbing.

I managed to pluck five mangos before I couldn't stand it anymore. I let go of the tree branch and, falling to the ground, began wildly to scrape off the ants that covered my body. They had left maybe a hundred tiny wounds in my skin, but I had won. I had five mangos. A hundred ant bites for some delicious mangos: it was a worthwhile trade.

But ants didn't always have to be a barrier to food. Sometimes they were our food itself. Some people would make ant pots, knocking the ants into a bucket of water and then covering it with banana leaves to keep them from crawling out. Once all the ants had drowned, they would soak them in vinegar until they were pickled.

We also roasted crickets and ate them hot and crispy. Millipedes, too, were crunchy when cooked well and could be eaten in a couple of hot and filling bites. Once I ate a grilled scorpion. I had to break off the head and suck out the meat much like you would from a lobster. And once we roasted a tarantula that turned out to have hundreds of ready-to-lay eggs clustered inside it swollen abdomen. We sucked these out with the rest of the meat. All of these things were just food for the stomach, something to stave off the endless ache of hunger. They weren't delicious. They were merely a remedy for the emptiness.

What I do remember being delicious was the snake. It was a python, about ten feet long. A group of grown men had caught it, sliced it into medallions and were cooking it into a soup with lemongrass and lime juice. When I tasted it, the meat was smooth and rich. It was the most delectable thing I had eaten in a long time.

The other treat that we were occasionally lucky enough to sample was rat. The field rats - big gray things with a plump pound or so of flesh on their bones - lived in holes under the corn fields. After the crops had been harvested, we would hunt them en masse, a swarm of children running into the fields with sticks. We would jab our sticks into the holes or pour water down them until the rodents came running out the other ends, where another child would be waiting with his own stick, ready to whack it. I never killed the rats myself, but I happily carried their carcasses back to the town where there was a woman who, for a small fee of a rat or two, would cook the whole batch. She would skin each rat with one graceful motion and then roast them over the fire. Then I could carry them home so that the whole family could gather around and pick their bones clean.

But all of this was illegal. All of it had to be kept secret. Because everything in Cambodia belonged to Angka. If one of the leaders, the Mei Kong, found out that we were stealing from Angka, that we did not trust Angka to provide all of our needs, we would be punished. Sometimes by beating, sometimes by death.

And yet every day, it seemed, Angka was growing poorer and poorer. Our rice portions were dwindling. The porridge was getting more and more watery. It was not enough.

To Keep the Light from Slipping Out

The hunger followed us around all day, every day. Sometimes, it became so strong, it grew a voice of its own. It whined quietly in my ears, a kind of whistling sound. A ringing. I tried shaking my head. I tried rubbing my ears. I tried blowing my nose. But nothing could shake the sound. Sometimes I would see someone speaking to me. I would see his mouth move, and I would know there must be a sound coming out. But I couldn't hear it. Not over the sound of the hunger whistling in my ears.

It wasn't until I sat down at the communal kitchen with my bowl of rice porridge, not until I had shoveled a few spoonfuls of rice into my stomach that the ringing faded. But it wasn't gone for long. I knew it would be back the next day.

At night we were quiet. There was nothing we could say to soften the ache of hunger in our stomachs. We didn't talk to one another as we got ready for bed. I didn't whisper to Thy as we lay side by side beneath our blankets. We didn't plan our next day. We only thought of the hunger.

And yet, some nights, when the moon was out, and the darkness of night was softened, we would come outside the hut and sit together as a family. We would gather under one blanket, if it was cold, and we would share our warmth with one another. And we would look up at the sky.

One night, we gathered beneath a full moon. It shone, enormous and golden, in the middle of a black sky. It was not afraid. It did not hide or pretend to be anything less than it was. It did not cower in the darkness. We looked up at its defiant beauty in awe, and for just a moment, it was enough. It was enough to forget the hunger. It was enough to believe that beauty was real. It was enough to hope. It was enough to remember a moon just like it, years before, when we sat on the roof of our home in Phnom Penh.

"When will it end?" my mother whispered.

"Will it ever go back?" Kann asked, his voice hushed like hers. "To the way it used to be?"

"Will it ever get better at all?" I asked.

"*Is* there anything better?" asked Thy.

Peou said nothing. She sat still, her arm looped around my mother's elbow, but she looked up at the moon whose light spilled a golden glow across her little face.

"I hope we're strong enough," I said it to the moon. Surely something so beautiful and bold, something strong enough to shine in a place like this, surely it could hear. "I hope we're strong enough to survive. Strong enough to make it to a time when things are the way they used to be."

"I hope…" Thy said. Her whisper, too, rose up to the moon. "I hope it gets better. I hope we have a better life."

"I hope we survive." My mother's whisper flickered up into the sky like the smoke of incense, thin and frail and vanishing.

But the moonlight was still there. Smiling. As though it could see something other than what we saw. As though it knew there was something out there besides night.

My father had been silent through all this, but he spoke now. "We don't know how this will turn out," he said. I shifted under the blanket, trying to sink deeper into its warmth, to feel the reminder of the bodies around me, that we were together. "Try to survive." My father

To Keep the Light from Slipping Out

spoke slowly, with emphasis. "Do what you must to survive."

We stayed there in silence, unable to tear ourselves away from the beautiful sight and from the luxury of warmth tucked under our blanket.

But one night, there was no moon. There was no light piercing the darkness. There was no reminder of beauty or of what could be. There was only hunger.

I crept into the milling hut after dark. Silently, I slipped up to the millstone where the workers had ground that day's rice grain before sending it to the communal kitchen. In the dark, I ran my fingers along the floor until I found a single grain of rice. And then another. And another. Once I had two handfuls of rice – as much as I could carry, I crept quietly back to our hut.

Inside the hut, I spread out my rice. I picked it clean of rocks and dirt, and then I scooped it into a tin cup with some water. I lit a small fire then. I had to keep it small because if they saw it, they would know. They would know what I had taken from Angka.

The moonless darkness was thick and heavy. My little flame sprang sharp and orange into the dark. I built a frail wall of banana leaves and coconut fronds to imprison this light.

My mother sat behind me, her body another wall to keep the light from slipping out into the night and betraying me. I don't remember anyone else being in the room.

Slowly the water warmed over the tiny flame. Slowly bubbles formed in the bottom and slowly they rose to the surface. Slowly it began to boil. The rice swelled, until at last it was done.

To Keep the Light from Slipping Out

I blew out the flame with a quick breath and the darkness engulfed us again. My shoulders sank in the relief of its safety.

In darkness, I ate the rice. Grain by grain. And in the darkness, I felt it. My mother's finger tapping gently on my shoulder.

This is the moment. The most terrible one. The one I would regret for the rest of my life. The one that still brings me to tears when I remember it. The one that clings to me like a ghost.

I knew what she wanted. She was hungry too. It was easier for us kids to find food. Easier for us to sneak, to creep through small places quietly. Easier to slip out during the day when the grownups were working in the fields. For her, it wasn't as easy. And of course, she, like the rest of us, was hungry.

But this is what I did: I kept eating. Grain by grain, I ate the rice I had gathered.

She only did it once more. Another tap on my shoulder. Again, I kept eating. I ate until the rice was gone.

And that was it. She said nothing. This was, I now know, her gift to me, perhaps the greatest one she could give. She said nothing. She didn't chide me. She didn't blame me. Her gift, as I ate the last grains of rice, was her silence.

But though she did not blame me, how could I not blame myself? I didn't then of course. I thought nothing of it at the time. But now, now that I know what would come after, how could I forgive myself?

Chapter 10

The Question I Couldn't Answer

I went on with my life as normal. That meant that I spent all of my waking moments thinking of food, looking for food, devising plans for acquiring food.

We were surrounded by corn fields, fields we worked every day, but the corn did not belong to us. It belonged to Angka.

But I didn't care about Angka. I cared much more about my stomach which whined every day for more. Desperate for more. So the first chance I got, I sneaked away. I ran to the fields and slipped behind their green veil.

The corn plants were still young at this time. Only a little taller than I was, though their golden tassels, which were at about eye-level, provided much less coverage than the thick green leaves below them, so I walked with my head bowed and my knees bent in order to conceal myself.

Because the corn was so young, its cobs were tiny, crisp, and sweet. I could peel away the papery husk and bite into it, cob and all. It was like eating a long skinny apple. In this way I disposed of the evidence. If I had come later in the year, the corn, full-grown, would have to be cooked, and I would have had to bring it home, giving the Mei Kong and her spies plenty of opportunity to catch me with my treasure. But they could not catch what was already in my belly.

The Question I Couldn't Answer

So I walked through the fields, slightly crouched, looking for the tiny cobs.

There was a deceptive kind of peace there in the corn field. The blue sky spread above me, vast and open. I could almost imagine that I could float up into it and away, anywhere I wanted to go. I could almost imagine I was free. And with nothing but leaves of green around me, I could pretend that there was nothing beyond this field. No soldiers, no guns. No empty rice bowls. No mound on the side of the hill concealing my little brother.

There was no wind that day. The stillness in the air felt like peace. But in reality, it was the stillness of the air that was my undoing. On other days, the wind swayed the corn plants with gentle hands. Movement flickered through the fields constantly. And any movement that could be seen, the wind took credit for. But there was no wind to take credit that day, and it must have been because there was no wind that my rustling through the corn leaves was seen.

I was only just finishing my second corn cob when I heard it. The rustling of leaves, one against the other. It was similar to the sound of the wind, but on this day, there was no wind. It came rushing towards me. And with it came the panic. This, too, was like the wind, roaring and unstoppable. I tried to run, but there was nowhere to go. I knew they had caught me.

And catch me they did. They pushed me into a small clearing – a brown patch of dirt where the corn had died. Four boys encircled me. They wore the same black pajama-like clothes that the soldiers wore, but they were too young to be soldiers. They were only a year or two older than me, but that didn't make them any less menacing. I knew who they were. The Mei Kong had

The Question I Couldn't Answer

plenty of spies like them. It was their job to catch thieves and traitors to Angka.

"What do we have here?" The biggest among them said, hoisting his machete over his shoulder. "A thief! Get down on your knees!"

I did what he said. What choice did I have? But I had little hope that my cooperation would get me anything.

He began to walk in a circle around me. The other three boys followed.

"A thief!" he cried again.

"Thief" the other boys whispered in response.

"You have taken what belongs to Angka!"

The boys murmured their agreement.

"You are *kmeng*!" He hissed the word. *Kmeng, enemy.*

They spat their contempt.

"What will we do with this thief?" The leader asked.

I could hear the flats of their machetes smacking into their hands as they contemplated this question.

"What will we do with this thief?" He asked again, and then he laughed.

It was a question that I, too, was contemplating. I was certain that they would kill me. I couldn't imagine anything else. The question was how. I knew of the ways that spies like these punished their victims. Would they break my neck? A machete to my head? Would they bury me alive so that I would die slowly?

They were silent now. I didn't hear a sound. Not their voices. Not their footsteps. Not their swinging machetes. I couldn't see their feet either. *Are they gone?* I asked myself. But I knew they couldn't be. I didn't dare look up.

The Question I Couldn't Answer

And then the leader boy's voice broke the silence with a hoarse whisper. "Thief!" he stretched the word out, long and slow. *Would they kill me?* I wondered.

"Stealing from Angka!" the other boys chimed in behind him, and they began their march around me again.

I had never been more afraid. And my fear took hold of me like a living thing. It gripped me and pulled me down into the earth, away from the boys. I knew they were there. I knew they were speaking. But I could no longer hear or see them. I was cowering down, deeper, deeper toward the grave into which I would surely descend.

Then I felt it. The machete against the back of my head. My skull vibrated with the impact of it. I was falling. And then everything was gone.

I woke up in the corn field. It was empty. Just me and the corn. I looked around. No spy boys. *Was it all a dream?* I wondered. *A hideous nightmare?* But then I felt an ache in my head. I reached back to touch my scalp and winced with pain at the bump that had welled up. *It was real.*

I stood there for a while, trying to understand. *Why? Why am I still here?* I was like the old woman back at the rice farm, this time pointing the finger at myself. *Why are you still alive?*

It was a question I couldn't answer. It troubled me as I ran home. It troubled me for a long time to come. The unexplained mystery. *Why didn't they kill me? Why am I still alive?*

It wasn't until years later that I would find an answer.

The Question I Couldn't Answer

I didn't tell anyone what happened. It was too frightening. Too horrifying. And how could I explain it?

For many months after that, I was different. I was afraid. I didn't take any more risks. I didn't sneak out to find food. I didn't steal. I didn't speak up. I was quiet. I hid. I didn't know why the spy boys hadn't killed me, and I didn't know that they wouldn't find me and report me. I didn't know that they wouldn't, somehow, come back to finish the job.

Chapter 11

The Thought Behind My Tears

The next thing I remember is my mother getting sick. She never complained, but we could see it. She wore it in her bones which showed sharply through her skin. In the clear angles of her cheekbone, of her jaw. In the sunken hollows around her eyes. In the frail line that was her body. Bones, with a delicate veil of skin.

She stopped going to the fields to work, but she still carried out her duties at home. She moved slowly around the hut, Peou clinging to the hem of her gray dress. Still graceful and smooth, but slow. Every day it became more difficult. One morning, she couldn't manage to lift the bucket of water Kann had brought in for the laundry. So she brought the clothes to the water and washed them there. Next, she told us the walk to the communal kitchen was too long, that she didn't have the strength. So she stayed home to rest while we went to breakfast, and my father managed to sneak a bowl of rice to bring back home to her. A few days later, she woke to find that she hadn't the strength to get up. She stayed in bed, awake but weary. It was like her illness scraped at her ruthlessly, peeling away her energy, her strength, even her flesh itself. Every day there was less of her. I watched her lying on the bamboo mat, the last hours of wakefulness having drained her. I watched her body mustering the strength to breathe the air in, and then to breathe it out again.

The Thought Behind My Tears

"Are you okay?" I would ask her.

She would smile and nod, but there was pain in the smile, and difficulty in the movement. She would lay her hand on my shoulder, as though I were the one to be comforted.

And then Angka called for me again. It needed my services at a child labor camp not far from here. This time, we were used to it. This time, we were not so afraid. Everyone acted like it was normal, the good byes.

"It's time for me to go now," I told my family when my bag was packed.

"Good bye, Thy. Good bye, Kann and Peou. I'll see you when I get back," I said to my siblings.

"See you later, Bong Sida," they said with hugs. Gentle touches of the arm around my neck, and then back to their daily tasks. It was a casual parting. Nothing sad. Nothing ominous.

It was the same with my father. "See you soon!"

Even my mother treated it as a routine parting, but I could see in her eyes that she was worried, that this slow stripping of her children – first Chun and Hong and now me – also stripped her of a piece of her soul. I could see that she didn't want me to go. I could see that there was something new, something desperate this time in her wanting. But there was nothing we could do to stop it. We had no choice. So she, like all the others, gave me a casual good bye. "I'll see you later, Sida," she said, even as her fingers lingered on my cheek.

It was as though we didn't know. As though we didn't realize the significance of this parting. And it would be easy to say we didn't, that we *couldn't* have known. But that isn't true.

The Thought Behind My Tears

Somewhere inside us, my mother and I, we knew.
"See you later, Ma," I said.

The camp was some five or ten miles away. I walked there with a group of kids from my town. It was a rice farm. I was taken to a long hut where I could spread out my bamboo mat and my meager pile of belongings alongside the mats of a hundred other kids about my age.

When I stepped out of the hut, it was like stepping onto the prow of a boat. All around rolled a sea of rice. The wind raced across it, whipping its surface into golden waves. The grain of the rice was yellow and ready for harvest. That was what they had called us here for.

Each day they lined us up across the edge of the field, and then we marched forward, each combing our own lanes for any rice that could be plucked. So all day, every day, I gathered up the stalks. All day, my fingers touched it, those golden grains. All day I waded through it, its stalks closing around me like water as I stepped. All day I was steeped in it.

And then at night, I slept in that hut, supported on an ocean of rice. For once, there was enough rice to feed us all. For once, I went to bed with a satisfied stomach. And yet, I lay awake at night, something more troubling than hunger gnawing inside me. Beside me slept a hundred other bodies, and yet I was alone. The sound of the breath of strangers rose and fell all around like the waves. I did not listen to their rhythm, though. My mind turned, instead, to the sounds that I wanted to hear. I thought of my mother saying my name as she kissed me on the cheek on my return from school. I thought the way she would wrinkle her nose as she pulled away. "Go take a shower, Sida! You stink!" It was almost enough to make me laugh, this memory. It was almost enough to keep me from remembering my mother as I had last seen her, lying on the mat, so frail. Almost. So I thought of my father. I tried to remember him on the rooftop back in Phnom Penh, holding his harmonica to his lips, and the sweet curls of sound that emanated from it. I tried to remember his voice, as he leaned over a chain of gold and explained to me how it was that he was fastening the link so that it would not break from the others. It had been so long since he had spoken to me like that. In that calm voice of a father who was passing on wisdom to his daughter. I tried not to think of him as I knew him now, a man in a world he didn't understand and couldn't control. Maybe he, too, was alone on an ocean, and he didn't know how to swim. What was there for him to do? It was with these thoughts each night that I sank into a troubled sleep.

    We were there at the rice farm for about a month, but then they released us, sending us home. A group of about twenty-five of us headed down a road that meandered its way toward Steang Chas. After we had walked a couple of miles, we came to a fork. About half of the kids went to the right, but the rest of us continued straight. We walked another mile or two and then another group peeled off – about seven of them this time, heading down a road to the left. When we came to another split, half of the kids followed the road to the left, and only three of us turned to the right.
    It reminded me of something, this slow dismantling of a group. I thought of the gradual slipping away of my mother's body. Of how layer by layer, she

was being stripped away from the inside out. The slow of the breaking of my mother's strength, like the slow breaking of our family. One piece at a time. The way her skin, almost translucent, clung to her bones. How thin and light she was and yet how heavy her body had seemed to be to her, the weariness with which she had lugged it across the room. She had carried that same weariness in her eyes when I saw her last, bore it in the gentle quiver of her voice as she said those words, "I'll see you later, Sida."

But she was sick.

"So sick." I found myself whispering the words. And at the movement of my lips I tasted them. Tears. They had streamed down my cheeks and moistened my lips. I tried to stop them, but I couldn't. I could only wipe them away with the back of my arm.

"What's going on?" "What's the matter with her?" I could hear the other girls' whispers beside me. But I didn't say anything. I didn't tell them that I was mourning. To speak the words aloud, I was afraid, might have made them real. When I had left, my mother hadn't said them. In fact, she'd done the opposite. "I'll see you later, Sida," she'd said. She had not spoken the thought that was behind her eyes. And so I, too, would not speak the thought behind my tears.

Still, I felt I had to get home. With every step I took towards our town, I felt it more and more urgently. I took the steps faster. Faster. The other two girls and their whispers fell away behind me until I couldn't hear them anymore. Faster steps. And faster. And then I began to run.

Back in Phnom Penh, I had been a good runner. I had won almost all the races. These were the same feet. I ran all the way to Steang Chas.

The Thought Behind My Tears

As I entered the town, I came to a cluster of three long huts. These were the hospital huts, and it occurred to me that my mother might be there. If her sickness had gotten worse, and surely it would have, then this is where she would have come. I stepped up to the first building and leaned in one of the windows. The room was full. Rows of cots, each filled with bodies, barely breathing, thin and shriveled like my mother's had been. I looked at each one for her familiar shape. The wave of her hair, the graceful lines of her hand. But I didn't see them. She wasn't any of these patients. So I moved to the next window and leaned in. I looked to the left and right. More patients lay on the beds, and I examined each one, but none of them was her. I went to the next window and the next, until I had looked through the whole building. She was not there.

So I went to the second hut, and I leaned in the first window. I looked to my right and my left, and then I moved on. When I had reached the last window, looked inside, and saw that my mother was not in this building, either, I stepped back, ready to move to the third hut.

"Oh!" said a soft voice. I turned, nearly bumping into a woman who stood behind me, but she didn't look angry. Instead, she looked at me with gentle eyes. "Are you looking for your Ma?" she asked.

"Yes," I told her.

But the woman's face dropped. It looked like my mother's had when she had said good bye. "I'll see you later, Sida," she had said.

"Your mother passed away three days ago," the woman said.

She might have said more, but I didn't hear it. She might have told me the details about how it happened. She might have told me my mother's last

The Thought Behind My Tears

words or whether or not she had suffered in the end. If she did, I didn't hear it. I didn't feel the tears pouring down my cheeks. I didn't feel the woman's palm as she reached out to stroke my back. I didn't feel myself lower to the ground.

Later - I'm not sure how much later -, I found myself seated on the ground outside the hospital, my face hot and sticky with tears, the woman's hand still moving up and down my back with gentle strokes. "You have to go home," she said at last. "Go home. Your father's waiting for you."

So that's what I did. I went home. My feet knew the way.

I returned to that same hut. The one whose post holes I had dug. The one whose roof I had woven with my father. I remembered the day we had built it. We had known we would live there. We had not known that some of us would die there.

As I stepped in the doorway, I saw a familiar figure. *Hong is home!* I thought with a sliver of joy I hadn't imagined possible a moment before. It had been months since I had seen her. She threw her arms around me with the tenacious grip that only sisters can have. This was what I had been missing all those lonely nights at the work camp.

My father was there, too. Peou stood at his side, her arm curled around his thigh. Bereft of her mother's, she had found the next best leg to cling to. My father put his arms around all of us. "Your mother has passed away," he said, his voice cracking under the weight of those heavy words. "Three days ago."

There were tears running down my cheeks, and tears running down Hong's, and tears running down the cheeks of my father. But we were together, a tangle of arms and tears and love. But even there, in the heart of comfort, I couldn't stop thinking, *But I didn't get to see her. We didn't get to say good bye.*

I thought these words over and over all afternoon and evening, and I thought them as I lay down my bamboo mat between my brother and my sisters. *I didn't get to see her*, I thought once again.

But then as night fell over us like a peaceful blanket, a new thought came to me. *What if she had eaten just a few more bites of rice? Would she have lived?* I thought of the two handfuls I had gathered that one night. I thought of her finger – thin and bony even then – tapping my shoulder. *I'm so sorry*, I thought. *I'm so sorry! I'm so sorry!* But it didn't matter how many times I thought it. I could say it over and over again for the rest of my life, but she would never hear. I could never tell her. And I could never erase what I had done.

Chapter 12

The Other Side of the Mango Trees

I woke up in a world that was emptier than it had been the day before. Or perhaps it was I who was empty. There was something missing. A whole part of my life, gone.

It's hard to move in a world that is so empty. Like trying to move in the vacuum of space, entangled in your own weightlessness. So it was hard for me to get up from my bamboo bed. To cross the floor of the hut. To walk down the road towards the hospital. To go around the side of huts into which, the day before, I had peered so hopefully.

Behind the hospital stood a row of mango trees. Even at the sight of them, my skin shivered. I could almost feel them, the ants from many months before, mandibles stabbing into my skin. Like an army of a hundred tiny, six-legged ghosts haunting me in the shadow of the mango trees.

On the other side of those trees, though, was the realm of ghosts far more sinister than those of ants. The dead were buried there. Those who died in the hospital. Many of them had no one left to give them a proper grave. No family members alive or well enough to dig a hole deep in the ground and to cover them thoroughly. For these, the hospital workers had to pull themselves away from their real jobs for a hasty burial, a thin shower of dirt over a corpse that no one had the strength to

The Other Side of the Mango Trees

mourn. It only took a little rain or a little wind to uncover a shriveled hand or bloodless face.

In such a place, I was certain, ghosts lingered long and angry. And it was said that if you saw its body, the ghost would haunt you.

But my mother was there, so my father had told me. He and Hong had dug her a grave, had laid her inside, spoken a few words, and covered her with a blanket of earth. I would be able to see her mound, he had said, rising a few inches above the ground around it, and I would know it by the small wooden post with which he had marked it.

I should go to her. I told myself. I wanted my feet to move. I wanted to be brave, to go to her grave. Maybe there I could tell her good bye. Maybe there I could say I was sorry.

But I couldn't do it. I couldn't bring myself to step into that world of the dead, where I knew I would see it, blue skin, rotting flesh, bodies emptied of their souls. Even my own mother, I was afraid, might have been uncovered. The wind blows, the rain falls, and the earth peels away from the dead. It could have happened to her. And I didn't think I could bear it.

I just stood there on the other side of the mango trees. On this side of death.

Harvest season had passed now, and the communal kitchen's supply was dwindling. We were, again, served small bowls of rice, or -worse- bowls of rice porridge with even smaller piles of rice settled at the bottom. If we wanted a full stomach, we had to find it ourselves.

I walked down to the river one day. I had done this many times before, having learned that some of the

The Other Side of the Mango Trees

best food scavenging options could be found on the banks of the river. On this particular day, I came in search of one of my favorites: snails.

The river was quiet. It was wide and gentle, moving along lazily as though it couldn't be bothered to hurry on its way to the sea. It had all the time in the world, because there was nothing that could threaten it. Trees grew around its banks, lush and green. It was a sunny day, and yellow light danced its way through the foliage and into bright splashes across the surface of the water.

I tied my scarf across one shoulder so that it hung against my side as a pouch, and I waded into the river. It was cool on my feet, slipping over my skin as though I was a part of it, as though I belonged there. I took a step deeper. The water was clear but dark. Clusters of green plants grew on its surface. Through their shadow, I could see their roots stretching down through the water. They might have had a few snails on them, but not many. They were too close to the mud. What snails lived there would be muddy and have to be cleaned. I knew I could find better.

I waded a little deeper till the water lapped around my waist. The current curled gently around me. Here, a few feet from the shore, the sun shone uninterrupted by trees and foliage. It spread warm across my skin and reflected across the shimmering surface of the water. Occasional green leaves floating along interrupted the orangish freckles of light dancing on the surface of the water. These were the plants I needed. I reached for the first plant, sliding it a few inches along the water and into the sunshine.

I only had to wait a second before I saw them. Three round shells dropped from the leaves and sank, down, down through the water. I didn't even have to be quick. I reached for them. One, two, three shells gathered in my hand. I held them up out of the water. These were big ones. About two inches in diameter, each. I tucked them into my scarf and reached for the next plant. When I moved it, two more snails quailed at the movement and dropped from the plant and right into my palm.

Before long, I had sixteen snails. It was as many as my scarf could hold. So I turned and waded back to the bank. I scooped them out of my scarf and into a little pile beside a tree root. Then I returned to the river.

It was a bountiful day for snails. Every plant I tried had at least two. I went from one plant to another, gathering snails until my scarf was almost full again. I was chest-deep in the water, and I reached out to a plant, lifting it from the river. Four snails sank into the water. I couldn't believe my luck. I stepped forward to gather them, but the riverbed gave way and I plunged under water.

The river was swirling around me, through my hair, my fingers, my nostrils. I didn't know how deep it was, how far beneath my feet it went, how far above my head. I only knew that it was everywhere, all around me.

I can't swim! That was all that my mind could register. *I can't swim!*

And then the inevitable conclusion. *I will drown.*

How could I have known? In that wild, swirling atmosphere so foreign to me, so unlivable, colors flashing, bending, spinning. Yes, water allows the light in, but it twists it until it is almost another thing entirely. Who could interpret it? How could I have known which way was up and which way was down? How could I know which way to reach for air and which way for death? How could I know which way led in an upward slope toward the bank and which led to deeper oblivion?

And whether the water above my head was an inch or a mile? Whether it was possible, worth reaching for, worth trying to break through, or if I lay, already enclosed in inevitable death? There was no way to know.

But I fought. I flailed. I grasped for anything I could get my fingers on. *The plants!* I felt their threadlike roots. The very homes from which I had sent snails fleeing. That meant I had found the surface. I reached for it, pulling the plants down under my fingers, desperate to pull myself up.

And for a second, I did. I broke into the air. Into the breathable. Into the clear, unsplintered light. And in that second, I could see the bank. I could see the line where water and the earth meet.

It was only a second. I was under the water again. But this time it was ok. I knew where to go. I moved in the direction of the bank, and my feet stumbled across the muddy river floor. I took another step, which propelled me upward, back into the air.

I breathed.

I spat river water.

I stumbled forward until my feet found dry land. I coughed and spluttered. I breathed.

The river was quiet again. A smooth surface, gently sliding towards the sea.

I checked my bag, only two of the snails remained tucked into its folds. All of the others had slipped back into the river. I sighed. It would have to be enough. I wasn't going back in the water again. Not that day. I walked back to the tree root where I left my first batch of snails and, gathering them up into my scarf, I carried them home.

We had to be careful how we ate the snails. If anyone saw us, they could turn us in for robbing Angka's rivers. So we waited for nightfall. When the hut was dark, I distributed them to my family members. One at a time, I would catch them in a corner and slip a handful of snails from my palm into theirs.

We were fortunate that it was a cold night. We lit a fire in front of the hut and gathered around it, holding our hands out to the warm glow, as though its warmth were the only thing that we sought.

There was a full moon again that night. Its broad silver light streamed down to greet our small orange one that flickered on the ground. Carefully, I tucked a snail under the glow of the flames, covering its round shell with a handful of ashes. Hong waited a moment before she did the same with hers. We didn't want to do them all at once and risk drawing attention. One at a time, the snails were buried in the heat.

There, with food roasting at our feet, and the light of the moon spilling into the darkness, we were able, again, to find hope.

"I hope," Thy whispered in my ear. "We have enough food."

"I hope we make it," whispered Hong.

"I hope we get out," I said.

Our whispers drifted silently into the sky to whoever would hear them. To whoever would see. To whoever had the power to do something.

Then we slipped our snails out of the ground and tucked them into our pockets. We went into the hut, into the safety of the darkness where we could pop their warm, juicy flesh into our mouths.

It was a feast that night.

Chapter 13

The Moment the Waiting Began

Hong was sent back to her work camp after that. We didn't know it then, but it would be a long time before we saw one another again.

Not long after she left, I got sick again. This time it must have been malaria. It came in waves. I would wake up feeling lethargic, but otherwise all right. I would linger in the hut while my father and siblings went off to work at their designated assignments in the town. I spent the morning resting, lying or sitting, and - when I could - sleeping. There was no one to talk to and nothing to entertain me.

Instead, I lay in the quiet of the hut, and I remembered the way things used to be. I remembered running through the streets of our old neighborhood back in Phnom Penh. I remembered my gleeful cry "Cockfight tonight!" I remembered the feel of the wind in my hair as I rode on Chun's back, my fingers tight around his shoulders. I remembered the eagerness with which I sprang out of bed every morning, impatient to discover what the day held.

She seemed like a different person, that Sida. Like someone who had died, but quietly. So we never got to whisper reverent words over her grave. We never got to say that we missed her. And yet she was gone.

The Moment the Waiting Began

And here was I in her place, lying immobile on the floor of the hut. I was imprisoned in my own body. Trapped.

I'm going to die, I thought, and I really believed it. *I'm waiting on a time bomb in my own heart*. I could hear it ticking inside my chest. Any second, I was sure, could be the last. Any second, it would burst under the load, and it would beat no more. But I didn't want to die.

So I did the only thing left to do. I prayed. "God help me," I whispered. And I hoped there was someone to hear.

But this was in the morning. The afternoon was different. Every day at about noon, something happened. A chill would begin in my bones and would creep through my body, spreading its icy grip until I was shaking uncontrollably, and my teeth shuddered in my mouth. I had to find a way to get warm. So I dragged myself out of the hut with my blanket, and spread myself out in the sun. But even the mighty sun with its brilliant rays could not warm my shivering body. I lay quaking and miserable, every muscle aching from the effort and the bruising of its own shaking against the hard ground.

It lasted for about twenty minutes, until a warmth finally stirred deep in my body and spread itself through my limbs. But then that warmth stayed, gathering itself into something hotter and hotter until I was sweating. I would muster what strength I could to throw off my blanket and trudge back into the shady hut. There I would lie, wilting in the fierceness of my own heat for about an hour until the fever began to recede. Then the chill would come back, rising again from inside, all the more brutal for the layer of sweat that coated my skin. If I could, I would drag myself back outside into the sun and brace myself against the terrible shaking.

The Moment the Waiting Began

This went back and forth all afternoon. Often my father would come home midday to find me this way. Peou, ever at his side, would watch as he held out to me a cup of soup, but I could not eat, not while I was in the grip of the chill or the fever. But in the evening, when he came home, the fever would have passed, and I would be hungry. He would bring a tin cup of rice and hold it up to me. I would prop myself up against the bamboo post and swallow a few spoonfuls of rice. But it was so exhausting, moving that spoon from the cup to my mouth. So exhausting, the effort it took to swallow. When I couldn't do it anymore, I set the spoon down. But my father, who sat by my knee, was watching me. "Eat some more," he said, nudging the spoon. So I would try. I would manage a few more bites before putting the spoon down again. My father would peer into the cup, at the rice that remained. "Finish it up," he said. "Eat some more, Sida. Try to get better."

I could see, as he said this, that he, too was tired. The weight of his work in the fields, the weight of his sorrow, the weight of his hunger, the weight of his desire for his children to survive, these things must have drained him of his strength as the malaria drained me of mine. It may be that the effort to speak these words "Eat some more. Try to get better," were as heavy for him as the spoonfuls of rice were for me. If he could muster the strength, then so could I. I finished the rice.

It happened again the next day. And the next. I would rest as much as I could in the morning, and in the afternoon, the chills and the fever would overtake me. Sometimes, my father would come home to find me in the sunshine in front of the hut. The fever had come, sweeping away the chills and drenching me in sweat, but I hadn't been able to muster the strength to get up and retreat to the shade. He would pick me up, then, and carry me into the hut. "It'll get better," he would tell me. "You will get better."

Sometimes, in the midst of the fever, I would feel a cool rush of air fluttering across my skin. I would look to see Kann beside me, a palm leaf in his hand, fanning the fever away. They took turns, Kann, Thy, and Peou, fanning me when I was hot. Tucking the blanket around me when I was cold.

One day, as I lay outside, wrapped in both blanket and sunshine, but trembling with cold, a Khmer Rouge soldier came by. I knew him by the tire sandals he wore and the hem of his black cotton pants. He stopped in front of me and said something to my father. My father came out of the hut to talk with him. I was too weary to listen to their conversation, but a few words slipped through to my ears. "Give her half," the soldier said. And then his feet shifted, and he walked away.

My father left for a moment. When he came back, he held something in his hand. It was half a pill, orange and semi-circular, like a tiny moon. He brought me a cup of water and held out the pill. "Take this," he said.

When I had swallowed the pill, my father lifted me and carried me inside. On the bamboo bed, I curled up under my blanket, still shivering.

That's the last I remember of the malaria. It seemed to vanish overnight. I don't remember taking the other half of the pill. I don't remember slowly emerging from the fever. I just remember being well again.

Now that I was healthy, Angka called for me to return to the rice fields. This time, I wouldn't be going alone. Thy and Kann, Angka said, were now old enough

The Moment the Waiting Began

to work in the labor camp. We packed our small bags, said good bye to our father, and walked away from the hut.

It had been the home of the Kong family. We had built it together, each one of us digging, lifting, tying it into place. But Hong and Chun were gone. My mother was gone forever. And now the three of us were leaving. The hut looked so empty with only my father and Peou at his side. She stood with one arm wrapped around his knee, the only body to which she could now cling. Is a chain of only two links a chain?

But while my father's hut became emptier, the hut at the camp seemed now much fuller. Kann and Thy set up their mats right next to mine, and I could sleep now, with the familiar sound of their breath, with the knowledge that they were only inches from me, that I was not alone.

Every morning the Mei Kong would wake us with a shrill whistle blow. "Wake up!" she would shout, marching through the hut, kicking our feet until we rose to get ready for work. After taking a few minutes to wash up and go to the bathroom, Thy, Kann, and I trudged off to work in the same rice fields. We weren't always given the same assignment, and we didn't always work side by side, but we were always nearby. It changes everything, when you know someone you love is nearby.

It was planting season, and it was our job, once again, to plant the rice sprouts pulled from another field into this wider one. One day, as we waded into the rice paddies, its dark water lapping around our knees, Thy pierced the silence with a shriek. "There's something on me! There's something on me!" She was leaping around in the rice, lifting her knees as high above the water as she could get them. I could see them only for a second,

The Moment the Waiting Began

she was moving so fast. The black blotches on her leg. I'd encountered them before.

"Go up, out of the water!" I told her, pointing to the dyke that ran the length of the field. I moved to it, and she followed, splashing and screaming.

We climbed up onto the dry earth. She could see them better now that she was out of the water. "Ew! What is that?" she cried. "What is it?"

"Calm down, Thy," I told her, looking around for a stick I could use. "They're just leeches." Glancing down, I saw that there were two on me as well. I would deal with Thy's first. I found a stick and carried it back to her. Thy was jumping and swinging her legs, trying to shake the leeches off. "Okay, stand still, Thy. Stand still." She tried, but even as she stood, she was shivering with horror. I slid the stick under the first leech and slowly moved it across its body to separate it from Thy's skin so that I could flick it onto the ground.

Kann had joined us on the dyke now, curious about all the fuss. He watched me work. When I started to pry the second leech off of Thy, Kann picked up his own stick and followed my technique to remove a leech from his own calf.

"They're so gross!" Thy whimpered, looking up at the sky, where there were no blood-sucking parasites to be seen.

The last leech on Thy's leg was big and glossy. I started at one end, peeling it away with my stick, but by the time I had reached the other end, it had re-stuck itself on the first side. "Kann," I called. "Come help me." So Kann came with his own stick, and together we were able to pry the thing from her skin.

"Is it gone? Is it gone?" Thy asked as Kann flung the slippery leech into the mud.

The Moment the Waiting Began

"Yeah," I told Thy. "It's gone. It's pretty bloody, though."

She looked down at the red streams that dribbled down her leg from the leech bites.

I flicked the leeches off of my legs with the stick.

"I'm not going back in there," Thy said with a shudder.

"Here's what you do." I reached around her ankle and tied her pant leg tight against her skin. "Now they can't get in." I tied the other one tight. "And keep moving. If you're moving they can't get a grip. If you stand still, that's when they latch on."

Kann held his legs out to me so that I could tie the bottom of his pants, too. Then he trotted back into the water, but Thy stood still. I tied my own pant legs tight. "Come on, Thy," I said, beckoning her. I waded back into the paddies. "You don't have a choice."

So Thy climbed down the dyke and back into the rice, but she eyed the water suspiciously, and with every sprout that she planted, she whipped her legs up out of the water, inspecting them.

We were much farther down the field when I heard her screaming again. She was dancing her way to the dyke. "It's on me, Bong Sida! I can feel it! I can feel it!"

So I followed her onto the dyke. "Right here!" she cried, pointing to her thigh.

"Okay," I said, untying the knot at the bottom of her pant leg and rolling it up. Sure enough, a glittery black leech had plastered itself just above her knee. It was a tiny one, this time, and I flicked it off with a stick. "Okay so sometimes, they're able to get through the pants," I admitted. "But not nearly as many."

The Moment the Waiting Began

"No," Thy said. She was shaking her head vigorously. "No, I'm not doing it." And with that, she walked away down the dyke.

"Thy!" I called after her, but she kept walking.

I returned to the rice paddies.

A while later, I looked up to see Thy walking along the dyke with a bundle of rice sprouts. She reached down, handing it to a worker whose sprouts had all been planted, and then turned to walk back down the dyke. She spent the rest of the day walking back and forth, delivering the sprouts to those of us in the water.

That evening, we gathered in the communal kitchen for our dinner. Thy and Kann sat next to me. We each had a bowl of stew, and we slurped its broth hungrily. "It looks like you found another job, Thy," I said between spoonfuls.

"I did," she said and took another scoop of stew.

We ate the rest of our meal quietly, sipping at the broth, but only the broth, draining our bowls dry until the best part remained: whatever was at the bottom of the bowl – rice, vegetables, sometimes even a piece of meat. This was how we always ate, saving the best for last, and then, when everything else was gone, savoring the experience of that last bite. Or sometimes, we couldn't even bring ourselves to do that. Sometimes it was too precious, too wonderful to be eaten and gone in a moment. On those occasions, we tucked it away in a pocket or wrapped it in a scarf to hide under our pillows or in the folds of our bags.

We weren't the only ones to do this. Many of the other kids, too, saved their most treasured food items, unwilling to give up the comfort of *having*. The knowledge that there was something precious in your possession. The girl who slept next to us in our hut did

The Moment the Waiting Began

it. I sometimes saw her at night tucking their bounty into her pillow.

One morning, when the Mei Kong had stomped her way in and out again, when we were just rising from our mats and stretching, a tiny wail burst out next to me. The girl was holding her pillow in her lap, her hands frantically patting the mat. "It's gone. It's gone!" she was saying. Tears were tumbling down her cheeks now, and her sister, who slept beside her, sat up and began searching the mat too. "No, it's gone!" the first girl cried, and put her hands in her lap. "Gone!"

The sister began to cry now, too. "My egg!" she whimpered.

"And the fish!" the first girl said. "Gone." They sat together and cried.

There was nothing we could do. We had to get to work or the Mei Kong would come after us. So my siblings and I rose and went out of the hut, the sound of their cries following us into the morning air.

That night as we sat at the dinner table, I ate all my stew. When Kann had drained all his soup and found a piece of fish at the bottom, I saw him unfolding his scarf in his lap. "No," I said. Kann looked at me in surprise. "Eat it now. Eat it all." I looked at the fish. "We don't know what will happen later."

I turned to Thy. There were some grains of rice still in her bowl. "Eat it now," I told her.

From then on, we ate all the food that was served to us. It was like my father had said that night in the moonlight. "We don't know how this is going to turn out."

And we didn't. We didn't know how it was going to turn out. And we didn't know how little we

The Moment the Waiting Began

knew. We didn't know it was about to change. Everything was about to change. Most of all me.

It happened that night in that same communal kitchen. Harvest season had come and gone, and the sizes of our portions were once again dwindling. I was just finishing my last grains of rice, leaving none to save, when he came up to me. I didn't know his name, but I'd seen him before. His family lived in Steang Chas, too. He didn't look at me, but his eyes kept shifting around, watching for the Mei Kong. That's how I knew there was trouble. He stepped close enough for me to hear him whisper. "I just came back from home. Did you know that three days ago, they called fourteen men to a meeting? One of them was your dad." *So what?* I wondered. *Angka called for meetings all of the time.* "They never came back," the boy whispered. "It's not good." And then he slipped away before the Mei Kong could see.

This was it. The moment the waiting began.

I froze there, holding my bowl. The world seemed to stop. It waited for me to understand. Sometimes Angka called people away for a task. Sometimes it didn't give them time to explain to their families. I wanted to believe this was what happened. But fourteen men? It didn't make sense. He had said it had been three days. Three days and he had not come back? I knew what it meant when Angka called for a meeting from which no one returned. It meant that those people were *kmeng*, the enemy. It meant they were doctors, teachers, wealthy, or traitors. It meant they had been found out. And I knew what Angka did with *kmeng*.

But I didn't know. I couldn't. Not really. After all, how many times had I faced what I was sure was

The Moment the Waiting Began

death? And I had cheated it. "Why are you alive?" the old woman had asked me.

I remembered the last time I had seen my father, standing in the hut with Peou. The hut had looked so empty without us. Now it was even emptier. Now it was only Peou. Peou was alone.

Peou was no longer the toddling child she'd been when we left Phnom Penh, her doll clutched under her arm. It had been almost three years. She had grown little in size, but she had grown older in other ways: quieter, more somber. None of these changed the reality of what she was. A four-year-old girl, fragile, clinging to her father's leg. Afraid. Always afraid of being alone.

And when I thought of Peou, something happened. Something very important. Something beyond just the waiting. It was when I realized that Peou was alone and that I couldn't leave her there. When I realized that there was no one else to save her. When I realized that it had to be me.

This is the moment my story shifts. Up until now, it has been a story of loss. The slow dismantling of a family. But there comes a time when pain shapes itself into hope. When brokenness gathers itself into strength. When death breathes and becomes life. When the rain falls, the winds blow, and then the things that were cut down begin to grow.

My mind was racing. *How can I do it? How can I get to her?* I could ask the Mei Kong for permission to leave. If I explained the situation, she might allow it. But what if she said no? Then she would know my intentions and would be watching me. No, I had to sneak away. It was too late now. It was already getting dark. I could never find my way in the night. Even in daylight,

The Moment the Waiting Began

I had never made the journey on my own. I fumbled through all of my memories of the path I had taken, of conversations I had overheard between adults. I remembered a woman mentioning the town, and the way she had pointed across the rice fields. That was all I had, but it would give me a place to start.

First thing in the morning, I told myself. *I'll go first thing in the morning.*

That night, as we settled onto our mats, I whispered to Thy and Kann. "Pa was called away to a meeting, and he didn't come back."

Their eyes grew wide, but they were silent. They knew we could not afford to be heard.

"Peou is there alone. I'm going to sneak away tomorrow. I'll go home and find out what happened."

"Is Pa safe?" Kann whispered.

"I hope," I said. It was all I could do. Hope. "I don't know. But if he is okay, he will find us. He will find a way. Don't worry about Pa. We just have to bring Peou."

They didn't say anything in response. They had to trust me. I was their Bong.

So I lay down on my mat. I had to fall asleep, knowing that my father was gone. I had to fall asleep knowing that out there across the rice fields, Peou might be falling asleep alone.

Chapter 14

The Last Place I Was Someone's Daughter

I woke with a start. *It's time! I have to get Peou!* But it wasn't time. It was still dark. Thy and Kann were still sleeping quietly beside me. I could feel their skin against mine. No, I had to wait.

I tried to fall back asleep. I needed all the rest I could get. I could lay my body still, but my mind was not so easily quieted. *What if they catch me? What punishment will the Mei Kong have for me?* The question marched back and forth across my thoughts until its rhythm finally lulled me into a fitful sleep.

I woke again. *Is it time?* But the hut was still silent. Darkness covered us like the mosquito nets that I knew hung over me but could not see. I laid back down and waited. I had never had to find my way to the village alone. *What if I get lost? What will happen to Peou then?* The words whined in my mind like an incessant mosquito in my ears. I fell asleep to them.

When I woke again, it was to the shriek of the Mei Kong's whistle. "Get up!" she bellowed, stepping into the hut. Her huge figure filled the doorway and she kicked at the first set of little feet. *It's time!* By the time she reached my feet, my heart was racing so hard it was difficult to lay quiet and lethargic, but I had to. I had to act like this was a normal day.

I rose slowly and stretched, and all around me, other children were doing the same. I scooped aside the mosquito net and followed the weary train of children out of the hut and into the morning light. We shuffled our way to the tub and waited our turns to splash the cool water on our faces. Then we dispersed into the bushes to pee.

    I crouched behind my bush, but when I was finished, I didn't walk back to the hut. I watched through the branches as the kids lined up. Thy and Kann joined the line. When the Mei Kong marched up to them, I waited to see if she would count. *Don't count! Don't count!* I pleaded. "Go!" she bellowed, and the line of little bodies lurched forward as they marched off to work. I waited until the last one was gone. Then I did as the Mei Kong herself had said. *Go, Sida! Go!*

    I broke into a run. The village was somewhere over there, on the other side of the rice paddy. Somewhere in the trees. I could see the tree line stretching across the southwestern horizon, a dark green haze probably five or ten miles away. I scanned the tree line now in the area where I remembered the woman pointing. There was a little notch, a tiny wedge of sky blue that sliced down through the jungle. I decided to make that my mark. Run towards the notch, and I would at least be close. Once I reached the trees, I wouldn't be far. Surely, I'd be able to find it then.

    I ran as fast as I could, trying to weave between the rice stubble. It had been months now since ground was submerged in quiet water, the rice green and tall and tender, but the fields had been harvested now and the water sucked dry by a thirsty sun. All that remained were the short, stiff skeletons of rice plants, stabbing up through hard, cracked dirt. I did my best to weave between the stubble, but when you're running, it's hard

The Last Place I Was Someone's Daughter

to be precise, and my bare feet stuttered onto their sharp stems more than once.

But I couldn't slow down. I had to get to Peou. She was alone. *What if someone comes and takes her?* I had to run. I had to run fast.

It was because I was running that I didn't see it. Something dark and withered, sticking up between the rice stubble. I almost tripped on it before I saw what it was, ten brown toes, or what was left of them, curled up and wrinkled, a worn pantleg dangling loose over each ankle. I tried to stop, tried to turn away. But I couldn't, not before I saw the whole thing, spread half-buried in a thin dusting of dirt, face upward to the sun.

And then I was running again, running away from that thing. It didn't matter how many dead bodies I had seen. They still struck me with a chilling fear every time. In Cambodia, they say that when you die, your ghost comes out of your body and lies there beside it, invisible. They also say that if you ever see a ghost, its evil will slip into you and drive you crazy. They say that ghosts come out at two times each day: at night and at noon. I looked up to where the sun burned down from high in the sky. I ran harder.

I ran until I could run no more, and then I stopped. Fear and panic shuddered down my spine. I wiped the sweat dripping from my face with my hand, but I couldn't wipe away the image of those ten brown toes.

Except for my ragged breathing, here it was quiet. No wind. Not a sound. Just the sky sagging down to the earth, hot and moist. Even the air was sweating.

I looked around at the miles of rice stubble. They seemed endless. Where was I? I looked behind me. Where was the corpse? What direction had I been going?

The Last Place I Was Someone's Daughter

It all looked the same, brown rice fields, and beyond them, jungle. Where was the village? I panicked.

Peou was somewhere in those trees. Alone. Scared. How would I find her now? And if I didn't find her what would happen? Maybe some other family would take her as their sister, their daughter. I would never see her again. Or worse. The Khmer Rouge might come and take her away.

Then I remembered. The notch. I scanned the tree line again. It had to be there. I found it! That piece of sky between trees. That's where our house was. That was where Peou was.

I began to run again. I ran until I could run no more, and then I walked. It was hot with not even a tickle of breeze to push the heat away. No sounds but my own breath heaving in and out of my lungs. And the flap of my feet against the earth.

I was alone. Peou was alone. Peou, who all this time had lingered, ever clinging to my mother's leg, and then my father's. Peou who never strayed from their sides, had been alone for probably two or three days now. *She must be so scared.* Even I was afraid to be alone at night. *And if I do find her, what will I do when I get there? I didn't ask permission when I left. What will they say when I show up with an extra kid tomorrow? How will they punish me?* There were no answers to these questions, but I didn't need answers. I needed to get to Peou.

When I was ready, I ran again. I ran until I couldn't. And then I walked until I could. It took me three hours to reach the jungle.

Winding between clusters of bamboo, I finally stepped into the gentle shade of Tamarind trees. I hadn't gone far before I came across a hut. It didn't look

The Last Place I Was Someone's Daughter

familiar, though. This wasn't our village. I crept around the side, through a grove of banana and papaya trees.

Then I saw an old man. He sat hunched on a bench, watching the birds flitting across the ground. He hadn't seen me yet. I could sneak back through the trees, and he would never know I was here. But maybe. Maybe he could tell me the way. Or maybe he would ask questions. Where was I going? Why wasn't I working? Maybe he would turn me in.

But I was lost. If I didn't ask him, I might never find the village before dark. And Peou was still alone.

I walked towards him. When he looked up, I asked as politely as I could, "Where do I go for Steang Chas Hospital?" A child could be looking for a hospital. She might not need papers for that. Then I added, "I'm going to see my mother." It sounded like a valid excuse.

But he didn't seem to care. He opened his mouth, dark with tobacco. "That way is Steang Chas," he said and pointed to the left.

I didn't wait for him to ponder it anymore. I sprang away in the direction he'd indicated. With every step I was getting closer to Peou.

The forest was quiet. I passed several huts but saw no one. It was as though the Khmer Rouge had put the forest to sleep. When I came to a path – only two brown ruts cut into the earth by an ox-drawn wagon, I knew I must be getting close. Then I saw the river, the quiet dark water brimming with the familiar green leaves. It was my river, the one in which I had nearly drowned just a few months before. I knew I was close, but it wasn't until I saw the long hut, the communal kitchen, that I knew exactly where I was. There were a couple of women gathered around the giant iron wok in the center. Their forms were dim in the shade of the hut. It would be hard for them to see me from this distance, let alone recognize me, but I couldn't risk it. I scampered off the cart ruts and hid behind a swath of green foliage. Creeping from tree to tree, I moved in the direction of our hut. This I knew well. The roof that we had built. The palm leaves that I had tied to the beams as I stood on my father's shoulders.

When I came to the doorway, she was sitting on the bamboo bed. She was just as I remembered her, tiny and fragile, her dark hair in tangles around her soft little dirt-smudged face. She sat perfectly still, her hands in her lap, her face blank, empty of hope. But when she saw me, she blossomed, eyes wide. I fell to my knees at the edge of the bed, and she began to cry. I wrapped my arms around her and felt the touch of her little body enclosed in mine. I was crying, too. Neither of us said a word. We only held each other. We were together. We were not alone.

We stayed that way for five minutes. But it couldn't last forever.

So I pulled myself up onto the bed beside her, and holding her little fist in mine, I asked her, "Peou, what happened?"

"We were in the kitchen," she began. "Eating. Two soldiers came in. They had a piece of paper. They called some names. Pa and some of the other fathers."

"Why," I asked. "Did they say why?"

"I don't know." Peou wiped her nose with the back of her arm. "They just said 'Come to the meeting.' Pa told me to go home when I finished lunch. So I finished my lunch and Pa, he got up with the other men. They went off to the meeting, so I walked home."

"What did you do when you got home?"

The Last Place I Was Someone's Daughter

"I waited. It got dark, but he didn't come back. I was scared. I was crying. I got the blanket, and I went to that corner. I put the blanket over me and waited." Her eyes grew wide. "Bong Sida, there was a wolf outside! I could hear him. He was howling and howling. And owls, too! I heard the owls. Bong Sida, it was so scary!"

She stopped to wipe more tears from her face.

"Then what happened?" I asked.

"I fell asleep. When I woke up, Pa still wasn't here. No one was here. I went next door. No one was there either. So I came back."

"Back home?"

She nodded. "I waited for him. At lunch time I went to the kitchen. I thought maybe he'd come back there, but I didn't see him. I got my porridge, and I came home. Then it was dinner time. He still hadn't come back, so I went to eat. He wasn't there."

"What did you do?"

"After that I stayed home. I was scared to go anywhere. I didn't eat. I just wanted to wait for Pa."

"Did anyone ask you to do anything?" I asked. "To go to work?"

"No."

"At night time, I was so scared." When she said this, her fingers squeezed tight around mine. "I'm so scared at night. I don't want to be alone. The wolves. And the owls!"

She started to cry again, and holding her hand was not enough, so I dropped back to my knees, and held her against myself.

"Don't let me go!" she cried into my shirt, her fists clinging tight to my back.

The Last Place I Was Someone's Daughter

And I didn't. I wouldn't. I would never leave her alone again.

When her sobs had slowed and her breath was even again, she sniffed. "Why didn't he come back?"

I stood up and wiped my own eyes. "I don't know."

I couldn't tell Peou what little I did know, not now. We had to get out of there. I began searching the hut, picking through the blankets and clothing.

"Am I going with you?" Peou asked.

"Yes."

They were hidden in the dirty clothes. Four pearls and a ruby, swaddled in cotton and wrapped in paper. Those would be useful for a bribe or exchange if we were ever in trouble. And then I found the picture of him. My father.

"But what if Pa comes back?" she asked. "And I'm not here."

"He'll find us," I told her. "He knows."

I wrapped the jewels and the photo in a ball of clothes, tied that in a blanket, and slung it over my shoulder.

"Come on, Peou." She followed me out the door.

At the side of the hut, we stopped by a bucket of water. Holding her fingers under it's cold surface, I washed the grime out from under them. There were dirt smudges on her cheeks and gunk in the corners of her eyes from nights of fitful sleeping and no one to help her wash up in the morning. With wet fingers, I wiped it from her eyes. We had to get out of there before anyone saw us. "Let's go."

I had always been Bong Sida, big sister. But now that title meant something new. Now it was up to me to take care of Peou. And not just Peou, but all of us who

The Last Place I Was Someone's Daughter

remained from the Kong family. Now it was up to me to make sure we survived.

I took my sister's hand and turned around to look one last time at the empty hut. The last home that I had had with my mother and father. The last place where I had been someone's daughter. But it was not my home anymore. No, there was nothing else that I needed from this place.

With Peou's hand in mine, we walked away.

Chapter 15

No Way Out

The walk back from Steang Chas was very different from the walk there. I knew the way now, and I didn't have to worry about getting lost. I wasn't in a hurry anymore. We could take our time. But most of all, I was not alone. I had Peou. We were together. And that was enough to make us happy.

We moved fast at first, eager to get away from the town and from any who would see us, but Peou soon got tired. We slowed down and walked at a leisurely pace. When we stepped out of the forest and into the rice fields, I lifted Peou onto my back to give her a break. She clung to me with little fingers, just like she had back in our kitchen in Phnom Penh when I had given her rides around the floor. She and Chao had taken turns on my back, laughing and squealing with delight. Somehow, in that moment, the old days didn't seem so far away.

We were alone in the rice fields. I could see to the horizon in all directions. Nothing but rice stubble and a distant tree line. It was just Peou and me. We couldn't help but feel the freedom of it. No one to make us work. To tell us where to go. To punish us if we didn't obey. No one to hide from. No need to pretend to be anyone besides ourselves. We were giddy with this freedom.

So when I put Peou back down on the ground, we began to skip. We made our way around the rice stubble with bouncing steps. Then we began to dance, her hand in mine, our feet moving in a playful rhythm. I remembered the old games we used to play on the streets of Phnom Penh, the hopscotch squares we used to mark out for our feet. So we began to hop on one foot then two, first my feet and then her smaller ones. We laughed as we hadn't in such a long time.

Then we began to sing because, feeling the way we felt, it seemed there was nothing to do but to sing. The only songs that we remembered were the ones that were taught to us to by the Mei Kong. So we sang about the glories of Angka and our loyalty to its cause. We didn't care what words were coming out of our mouths, only that our lungs were filled with breath and joy, and it was bubbling up in song.

When we finally reached the camp, the sun had set, and darkness was just beginning to slip across the sky. This darkness helped us to slip, ourselves, unseen into the hut. Dinner had already come and gone, and Thy and Kann were settling onto their mats under our mosquito net. Peou and I slid in beside them as though this were the same as any other night, as though we were just coming in from the bathroom, as though Peou had been with us all along.

Thy and Kann pretended, too. Their eyes were wide, and smiles trembled behind their lips, but in every other aspect, they behaved casually. They could not hug us. They could not cry out their relief. They could not grasp Peou's hands with celebratory fingers. Instead, we huddled close under our mosquito net, so close that our skin touched. In this way, we could rejoice. We could feel the physical reality that we were all here. We were together.

Then Thy slipped a hand under her pillow and brought out a small cup of rice. She must have set it aside during her dinner and sneaked it out of the

No Way Out

communal kitchen. Kann, too, pulled out a handful of dried fish. They held these out to Peou and me. We ate them quickly and quietly.

Then we lay down to sleep, Peou nestled between Thy's body and mine. As though she had always slept there. As though she belonged.

That night as I lay there, with all of my younger siblings together, the sound of their breathing was the sound of peace. But slowly, the relief, the joy, it started to slip away. In its place, worry began to slide in. *What will they say when they see Peou in the morning? What will I tell them when they ask who she is?* And then the most chilling thought of all. *What if they find out who we are?* I remembered my father's warning, never to let them know. The deeper we sank into the night, the more and more sure I was that this was what had happened to him. They had found out who he was.

When I finally did fall asleep, I fell into a nightmare. I was running through the forest. Branches and vines tangled themselves at my feet and clawed at my legs, but I broke through them. I would not stop. I couldn't. Thy was beside me. She was running, too. We were breathing hard, running as fast as we could. There were two other girls beside us, too. We were all running. I could hear the rustling of leaves and branches behind us. I looked over my soldier to see them. Khmer Rouge soldiers, dressed in their black cotton and their tire sandals. They were chasing us, and they were bigger, faster. "Stop!" they cried. "Stop!" But we didn't stop. I would have rather died than go back to them. To torture or execution. We kept running. But they were gaining on us.

And then suddenly we ran into a wall. It stretched high and wide. There was no way out. We

No Way Out

were trapped. I looked at Thy, at the terror in her eyes. They were going to catch us!

I woke suddenly. I was breathing as heavily as I had been in the dream, and my heart was racing as fast. I lay still a few moments, and I let the fear drain away. Morning was just beginning to let its slender threads of light through the thatched walls. I felt a small shape beside me and remembered that Peou was here now. I remembered that my father had been taken away. I remembered that we were in danger.

There in the frail morning light, when all was quiet, I prayed to whoever would hear me. There was nothing else I could do. There was no way I could save us. There was no way out. I could only hope that there was someone out there, and that that someone would hear me and would do something. It was the only thing left to hope for. *Please,* I begged this someone. *Please don't let them see her. Please.*

Gradually, the light swelled. It warmed into day. And outside, the whistle shrieked, as it did every morning. The Mei Kong came in. "Get up!" she shouted, kicking at my feet.

I sat up right away, nudging Peou to do the same.

The Mei Kong peered down at us from where she stood, tall and fat.

My heart began to race again, just as it had in my dream. *Please,* I prayed again. *Please don't let her see Peou. Block her eyes! Block her eyes*!

The Mei Kong stepped over us and moved down the hut, kicking at the other children's feet.

I exhaled. I tried to breathe normally. Tried to slow my heart. I took Peou's hand and led her out the door, Thy and Kann following just behind.

No Way Out

Once we had used the bathroom, we lined up on the road, ready to head into the fields. Peou stood between Kann and me. When the Mei Kong stepped up to the line, she pointed her finger to the first child. She began to count. *Please don't let her see Peou,* I prayed again. As she walked down the row, nearing us, my prayer grew more and more fervent. *Block her eyes! Block her eyes!* I begged. The Mei Kong stepped right past Peou and kept counting. When she reached the end of the line, she took a deep breath, "Go!" she shouted at us. "Go!"

I had never been more delighted to be sent into the fields.

I found myself praying the same prayer throughout the day: when we lined up to get lunch, when we stepped forward to return our empty plates, when we filed into the Khmer Rouge meetings. But if they saw Peou, they didn't notice that she was new or that she was too young for this camp. They acted as though nothing had changed.

When I lay down to sleep that night, I felt relief. We had made it through the day, and no one had noticed Peou. Now, I hoped, it was too late for anyone to notice. We would continue to be quiet, not to stand out. Just like my father had said.

But when I fell asleep, I fell into the same nightmare. Thy and I were running with two other girls, tearing through the forest, the soldiers on our heels. We ran until we stumbled into the wall. There was no way out.

I woke again in a sweat. *There's no way out! There's no way out!* I couldn't silence the words that still ran through my mind.

No Way Out

Peou slept quietly beside me. So did Thy and Kann. We were safe. For the moment.

Still, I had the nightmare every night. Every night I ran from the Khmer Rouge, and every night they cornered me against a wall. Every night I was trapped.

And then one morning I woke up, and I knew something was wrong. The nightmare had been the same. And as always, my heart was beating hard and loud, and my skin was covered in sweat, but that was not what troubled me. Something was missing.

I looked around the hut, and I noticed that the mat next to ours was empty. That mat belonged to two sisters, about the age of myself and Thy. They were the ones whose egg and fish had been stolen a few months before. The ones who had cried such bitter tears at their loss. Now their mat lay empty. Their bags were gone.

I tried to tell myself that they might have woken early and gone to the bathroom. But I knew that was unlikely. None of us went out in the dark for fear of the ghosts who roamed in great number ever since the Khmer Rouge had come.

I waited until morning when the Mei Kong woke us, and we gathered to work. I looked for the two girls in the line, but they weren't there. I looked for them in the kitchen at meal time, and I looked for them again at night when we returned to the hut, but they were gone. We never saw them again. *I knew it,* I thought to myself. *They always spoke so primly. They seemed so delicate. They must have been rich before. They were like us. They were found out.*

It happened again, a few nights later, I woke up in the morning and noticed another family missing from

No Way Out

the hut. There were three siblings this time. They had been there when we had gone to sleep, I was certain. But now, they were gone. We never saw them again. No one said anything. We didn't dare. "Don't do anything to draw attention to yourself." I remembered my father's warning. And so I said nothing.

But I was afraid. I was more afraid than I had ever been before. The fear haunted me all day as I worked in the fields, as I ate my rice. It hovered behind me. It leaned over my shoulder. But at night, when I slipped in under the mosquito net and laid myself down next to Peou, the fear leapt upon me, strangled me, pinned me against the mat, paralyzed me. *They are going to come for us. They are going to find us. They will take us away.* I wasn't afraid to fall into the nightmare anymore. The nightmare was no worse than the waking world. We had run into a wall. *There's no way out! They will find us and kill us. There's no way out!*

I remembered the old saying: you can cut the grass above the ground, but rain will fall, winds will blow, and it will come back alive. If you want it gone, really, truly forever gone, you have to dig out the root.

They had found my father, but it wasn't enough to kill him. They had to come back for the root. I knew what the root was. It was breathing peacefully by my side. Peou's little hands. Thy's peaceful face. Kann's curled body. My own trembling one. We were the root. And the Khmer Rouge knew this. They would come looking for us. They couldn't afford to leave anyone behind, anyone who might grow up to avenge their family. They had to tear out the root. They would find us in the night and take us away. And just like with the others, no one would say anything. They wouldn't dare.

No Way Out

I didn't know at the time that this was happening across Cambodia. Pol Pot, in the height of his power, had grown fearful of even his own allies. Suspicious that they may become rivals, he had ordered a purge of not only "the new people" but also whole swaths of the eastern faction of the Khmer Rouge. Even as children were disappearing from my hut in western Cambodia, mass graves were being filled in the east. Pol Pot was striving feverishly to dig out the root.

I did not know this. I only knew terror. I lay still, choking in it. How could I fall asleep, knowing that they would come, any minute they would come and steal us? There was nothing I could do. *There's no way out! There's no way out!*

But even then, in the middle of paralyzing fear, I remembered something. I remembered the warmth of my mother's palm, spread against my back. I remembered her sorrow that she could not protect me anymore. I remembered her words "If you are ever in trouble, Sida, pray to God. He will help you."

I still wasn't sure if there was anyone out there. And if there was, I wasn't sure He would hear me. But I had prayed when I was sick, and I had been healed. And I had prayed that they wouldn't see Peou, and they hadn't. And there was nothing else I could do. There was no way out. So in the darkness of the hut, I did it again. I prayed. *God, protect us. Keep us safe.* Once I had prayed those words, there was nothing else I could do. I let sleep take me.

When I woke up in the morning, we were still there. Peou, Thy, and Kann, we were alive. For one more day.

For a while, every night was like this. I would lie down in the darkness, and the fear would seize me, and I

No Way Out

could not sleep, not until I prayed. *Please protect us!* But once I had said those words, the fear would loosen its grip around me, and I would drift off.

Every night I still had the nightmare, and every morning, I still woke with my heart racing. Each time I woke, I checked. And each time, my siblings were all there.

The others were not all so fortunate. One morning, I woke to find that another family had disappeared. Two brothers. The fear returned to me, as strong as ever, but as I lay down that night, I lifted my prayer into the darkness. *Protect us, please. Keep us safe.* It rose, invisible, into the air above me. It drifted out into the night.

That night I dreamt, again, that we were running from the Khmer Rouge. Thy, two other girls, and I. We ran as hard as we could. We splashed through mud. We sprang along the banks of a pond. We scrambled through bushes. Our bare feet were coated in mud and scratched by the branches, but still we ran. "Stop!" the soldiers behind us yelled. "Stop!" But we would not stop. We had to escape.

Then we broke out of the trees, and there was the end. But this time it wasn't a wall. It was a cliff. We slid to a stop, and we looked at one another. The soldiers were coming. We could see their black uniforms through the leaves.

I looked down. It was a long fall, hundreds of feet. We could never survive it. But the soldiers were coming. And I would have rather died than go back.

Together, all four of us at once, we turned away from them and we leapt.

No Way Out

The moment that my feet left the ground, I was weightless. The earth itself was gone. There was only sky. And I was part of the sky.

I was terrified. I was falling. I knew I was going to die. But there was something else. I was free. At last, I was free.

And then I woke up.

As with every other night, I was shaking, my heart racing, my clothes drenched in sweat. But this time it was different. This time I didn't feel trapped.

Chapter 16

They Are Already Dead

One day, we were given the afternoon off. I don't remember why or what the exact circumstances were. What I do remember is that I had overheard some boys in the camp talking about the "Number One Force" camp nearby. They had motioned in its general direction and mentioned that it was about an hour's walk, just north of the big palm tree. I knew that "Number One Force" meant teenage boys, and when I heard the phrase, I immediately thought of Chun and wondered if he might be there. So as soon as our afternoon of freedom began, I headed straight for the big palm tree. It was only a vague hope. A mere possibility that Chun was there. But for even a small hope, it was worth it.

So I walked up the road, and when I reached the palm tree, I turned right and walked a while more. At last I came to a camp, a cluster of huts, much like ours. It was quiet. I don't mean that it was empty but still. There were many boys there, taller than the ones at my camp but just as thin. And yet though the place was full, there was almost no movement. They must have had the day off, too because they sat motionless in the afternoon breeze. In spite of the presence of so many young men, the camp felt like a ghost town.

I walked between the huts peering closely at each silent boy that I passed to see if he was my brother. Then I looked up, and there he was. He was only a few feet away from me. He stood, leaning against the wall of a hut, a tin cup of water in his hands. He looked different, so different than the Chun I remembered. His bones were sharp and angular. His chin long and pointed. And he was thin, so *so* thin. But even so, I knew him. I knew this boy to whose back I had clung on all those bike rides, whose bed I had snuggled into as he read after bed time, who had carried me across the irrigation ditches when I was paralyzed. I knew my bong.

He knew me, too. When my eyes met his, he was already staring with an astonished face. His eyes filled with glossy tears, and his lips quivered in something almost a smile. And both of us, for a moment, were breathless. Who needed breath when a long-lost sibling was so close?

I ran to him. I say "ran," but it was only a step or two, he was already so close. He reached forward a hand, and I grasped it with mine. Two golden links, fastened together again.

He looked down at the tin cup in his other hand. "You want some water?" He spoke the words quickly as though we were running out of time, but we hadn't yet found any other words to say. What could we say?

So I answered, "Yes," because the word was available. So he quickly scooped another cup of water from the tank and offered it to me. Then we sat down on the ground beside the hut, and I drank.

Chun told me about work in this camp, how they hacked at the earth with hoes and then carried the rocks to wherever the Khmer Rouge needed them. It was hard heavy work, work reserved for this, the "Number One Force." As he talked, I noticed the scars on his boney legs. Wide gashes slit across the calves where the hoe must have slipped on the rock and landed in his flesh instead. Some of these were still fresh and pink, still struggling to heal.

They Are Already Dead

When he finished, I knew it was my turn to give an update. I took a deep breath. "Did you hear about Ma?" I asked. Right away, I knew that he had. He nodded, his eyes on our feet. There was nothing more to say about it.

So I took another breath and asked the next question. "Did you hear about Pa?"

Now, he looked up with wide eyes, and I knew that he hadn't. So I told him everything. I told him what the boy from Steang Chas had told me. I told him that he said it had been three days. I told him that I had come back the next day for Peou, and that Pa had still not returned.

He was quiet for a minute, thinking. "Three days?" he asked.

"Yes," I said. "Do you think he could still be…?"

We knew the chances were slim. And yet we couldn't bear to give up hope. Because maybe, just maybe, he had escaped. Or maybe they really had just called him away to work somewhere else. It was possible. And as long as it was possible, we couldn't help but hope.

"Maybe," Chun said. "But you can't say anything about it. Don't ask any questions. You have to keep quiet." He reminded me of my father then, as he gave me that same warning.

I nodded and looked down. His legs were thin, so thin – skin stretched across bone, but his knees were big and round, much wider than his calves or thighs.

"Why are you so thin?" I asked. "They're not giving you enough food?" I would have thought for their Number One Force at least, they would be able to find enough.

They Are Already Dead

"Sometimes," Chun answered. "But you know, they make us work so hard." He breathed out heavily, the weight of all those loads of rocks hanging in his breath. "Sometimes there's enough food, and sometimes there's not, but we lost so much weight, so much muscle before, now even when we eat enough, we can't gain it back." He looked off into the distance as he said it again. "There are some losses that you just can't retrieve."

I thought about this as I looked around the camp. The other boys still sat silent and motionless. The wind flickered by, and their shirts and pant legs fluttered gently with it, but their bodies were unmoved.

"It's like they're dead," I whispered to Chun.

"We are," he said back. "We're like corpses without a spirit. Breathing, but no mind. No reason to live. Sometimes, when we have food, they don't even feel like eating anymore. We have no hope, so why eat? They slowly die of hunger, but not because there isn't enough. I can't do anything about it. There's no hope here." The wind flickered through his own hair. It was long enough to cover his scalp, but haggardly chopped. "They are already dead."

"What's going to happen now? It seems like everyone is dying." I asked him because he was my bong. He was the closest thing I had to a father, and if he didn't know, then who would? "What's going to happen?"

He shook his head. "I don't know." Then he looked at me with those sad eyes. "Keep safe, Sida," he said. "Keep them all safe. If it gets better, we'll find each other."

This was a nice thought. Finding each other. So we let that thought linger in the air.

They Are Already Dead

We didn't say anything else for a long time. We sat silently near to each other. It had been so long since we'd been able to be near. I gazed at his face. His eyes that had once been filled with laughter and mischief. He probably saw the same in mine. Eyes that once had been. And I had hope, as I looked at them, that one day they would be again.

I stayed as long as I could. Just being near him. But the sun was reaching its way towards the horizon. I needed to leave in time to be back at the camp for dinner. "I have to go back," I said in a whisper because the whole world now seemed so quiet.

We stood up and came together, side by side. My arm linked its way around his, and my side clasped itself against his. "Keep safe," he told me. "Remember, Sida, be quiet. Don't stir anything up," he said because he remembered the way I used to be. He had seen so little of the Sida that I was now. "Just keep everyone safe. Do what you can to make it through."

I nodded, but I didn't step away. Not yet. I couldn't bear to. The pressure of his arm against mine. The warmth of his body. I didn't want to leave it. Not yet.

"Good bye," I said because I had to. But still I stayed there. With my big brother. My bong.

"I'll see you," he told me. "I'll find you."

With those words, with that promise, I was able to break way, to open my grip and slip my arm from his, to break the link, and to walk away.

I didn't know, then, that it was the last time I would see him. I wouldn't know for many, many more years. Just as with my father, I never did find out exactly what happened. The hope was never crushed in a final blow. It just slipped away in pieces over the years. Year after year of never hearing from them. Year after year of looking but finding nothing.

So it's only that final promise that he made me which allows me to know for sure. It's only because he had said so firmly that he would find me, that I know. Because he didn't. And if after all these years he didn't find me, there's only one explanation.

But I didn't know that, as I walked away. As I walked away, I had hope. I had finally seen him. For the first time in over a year, I had seen my bong. I had held his hand. It seemed the world was getting better. It seemed that the chain might link itself back together after all. It seemed that those of us who were left might still be a family again, that we might all be together at the end.

And in that moment, as I was walking away from my brother, another kind of hope was brewing. This, too, I didn't know and wouldn't know for years. Hundreds of miles away on the other side of the Vietnamese border, forces were gathering. The remnants of the eastern faction of the Khmer Rouge who had fled Pol Pot's purge had joined with their communist allies in Vietnam. They were planning an invasion.

Chapter 17

What Hope Sounds Like

It wasn't long after my visit with Chun that they shut down our labor camp. Angka decided it had no more need for us in these rice fields, and the Mei Kong told us all to go home.

But we had no home to go to. I didn't point this out to the Mei Kong. I remembered my father's warning and Chun's, and I did nothing that would draw attention to us. So when the other children left, each going to his own family, we followed a cluster of them. They led us to a small town not too far away.

It was another farming town, one with fields of yams, yucca, corn, and tomatoes. They were in planting season, so the fields looked bare and empty, but beneath their soil, seeds were breaking forth into life. Very soon, they would burst into the air, green and growing fast.

We when registered in the town, they asked me my name.

"Mann Sida." I told them. Mann was my father's middle name. I remembered how my father had never given them our real surname. Every time we went somewhere new, he had given our name a slightly different twist. I knew that it was more important now than ever. We could not let them trace us back to him

"Where are your parents?" they asked. I pretended to be confused. After all, they had told us that Angka was our real family. "Your mother?"

"She died," I told them slowly, like it was hard to put the pieces of my memory together.

"Your father?"

I shook my head like I didn't know. Like trying to recall these things was difficult, painful.

Then they waved me away and moved on to the next person in line.

I led my siblings into town, feeling confident that they would not find us here. We came across an empty hut, which we decided to make our own. The hut had been empty for a reason. Its roof was unraveling. In some places, the fronds had come untied and hung limply. In others, there were gaping holes where the roof was missing all together. It was a fitting roof for our family. Incomplete and weary. And yet clinging to what remained, doing its best to be whole.

As we lay down under this fractured roof, we could see pieces of sky. Black and flecked with tiny lights. Stars.

When the rainy season came, we had to abandon our hut and instead spent our nights in the communal kitchen where the wind sometimes blew in gusts of rain but was otherwise dry. The floor was too muddy for us to sleep on, so Peou, Kann, and I slept on the kitchen table, while Thy stretched out on a wooden bench. The table was tight, though. There was no room to curl my legs, not without pushing Kann off the other side. And yet the table was shorter than I was, so my feet always hung, restless, over the side. I often worried about falling off the edge in my sleep.

We weren't there long before I woke up in the night with a feverish itching on my back. I sat up and scratched it but as soon as I did, the itch moved farther down my spine. So I scratched the new itch. Again, it moved, this time towards my shoulder. It seemed like there was a parasite crawling under my skin. I chased it all around my back with my finger nails until my skin was torn and bloody, and I was so tired, I couldn't scratch any longer, so I fell back asleep. In the morning, I woke to a tender back and bloody finger nails, but the itch was gone, and I considered this a real improvement.

The following night, it happened again. I woke in the night to find that the itch had spread across my armpits and chest. Again, I chased it with my finger nails, scratching until my nails were crusted with blood. And again, I fell into an exhausted sleep. On the third night, I went to bed prepared. I kept a broken piece of brick at my side when I slept, and when the itching woke me, I grated it with the brick until my fingers were too tired to move.

I kept this up for a couple of weeks before an old woman in the town, seeing my lacerated skin suggested a remedy. That night, I woke and scratched the itch as usual, tearing at my skin till it broke. Then, I spit on my fingers and rubbed the saliva on the open skin. Immediately, I could feel it. The cool relief. I did this all over my back and chest, everywhere the itch had been. Opened it till it bled and then filled it with my own spit. I fell back asleep.

That was the last night I ever felt the itch. It was gone.

The rain came to an end soon after that and we moved back into our partially-roofed hut. Back to sleeping under the stars.

We spent our days working in the fields, serving Angka by planting seeds. And every evening, Angka fed us in the communal kitchen. At night, we slept in our hut. Four of us lay down in a row on our mats. A chain with four links. Darkness fell over us. And the stars came out, punching holes in the darkness. I thought of my bong - Hong and Chun - and imagined them here with us. I imagined us all together again.

As I lay there thinking, a sound punctured the silence of the night. Boom! It was a sound I hadn't heard since we had fled Phnom Penh. And then it rang out again in a long stream of gun shots. Boom-Boom-Boom-Boom! The sound was distant but clear.

A shiver ran across my body, and my skin puckered into goosebumps. My heart's pace quickened, and I lay awake long after the silence had closed back over the night. It was not fear that kept me awake. It was hope. Gunshots meant fighting. And fighting meant change.

I heard them again a few nights later. Only a few shots punching holes in the silence. I listened hard, trying to hear where they came from. I wanted to know in which direction our hope lay.

It was around this time that I began to hear other families speaking of the labor camp for teenage girls nearby. Just as with Chun's Number One Force camp, I heard about it only in snippets. A gesture pointing in the general direction. Some phrases here: "that work camp" and "the young ladies." A couple words there: "east" and "close."

My recent visit to Chun had given me such hope. It was fresh in my mind: the image of our arms linked. Not just his and mine, but all of us, the Kong children together again.

So one afternoon when we finished up our work in the fields, I slipped away early. I ran down the road in the direction I guessed it to be in. When my legs grew tired, I slowed to a walk. It must have been an hour or so before I reached it.

What Hope Sounds Like

The teenage girls' camp was so different from the boys'. Like the boys' camp, it was full of hundreds of teens, but this one was a bustle of activity. Their work day had ended, but the girls were busy and moving. I saw several of them crouched over a tub of water, vigorously washing their clothes. Some squatted outside, stirring pots over small fires. Some could be seen inside their huts, sleeping, but the air was filled with the quiet chatter of young women.

When I found Hong, she was sitting on the ground outside a hut. There was a small pot in her lap, filled with strips of something pink and slippery. She was just pushing one into her mouth when she looked up and saw me. "Sida!" she cried, pushing the pot forward so she could stand up. "You've come?" It seemed a genuine question. Like she really wasn't sure if I was standing there or if I was an apparition. "You've come here?"

"Yes," I assured her, putting my arms around her in a hug, further confirmation that I was flesh and blood. "We live close by now," I told her, pointing in the direction of our town.

She nodded. "Sit, sit." So I did. She held the pot out to me. "Want some?"

I picked a pink strip out of the pot. It was thin and rough, but there was plenty of it. "What is it?" I asked as I began to chew.

"Yucca skins," she told me, popping another one into her mouth.

"Where did you get it?" I asked, looking around. It felt strange to eat out here in the open where anyone could see.

"The kitchen. They were leftovers that were being thrown out." She shrugged. "It fills the stomach."

"But won't you get in trouble?" I whispered. "Everyone can see you."

"It's not stealing." Her voice was firm. The same voice that used to tell me to do my chores. "They were throwing it out. They don't mind."

So I took another piece and ate it. It didn't have any flavor, and its texture was course, but she was right – it did fill the stomach.

"So you're not in Steang Chas anymore?" she asked through a full mouth.

"No," I said, and I told her about our father's disappearance. I told her how I had gone to get Peou, and how the four of us had been together. I told her how, when the camp disbanded, we had no home to return to and how that had brought us to the nearby town.

"Oh," Hong said when I was done. "I didn't know."

She was quiet for a moment, looking off in the distance.

"And you?" I asked.

"Hungry," she said, still looking off. "Always hungry. There's never enough food." Then she looked down at the pot. There were two yucca peels left. We each took one and ate it.

"I don't feel well." She spoke quietly, her face troubled. It was the same look she used to make when she saw the way I had soiled my school uniform back at home, like she was disturbed that there could be such disorder in the world. How little we knew, back then. "They work us so hard. Carrying heavy loads, day after day. And sometimes they have us in the fields, planting, harvesting. The corn fields—" she stopped suddenly and was silent.

What Hope Sounds Like

I looked at my sister. Her face was dark, a strange shade of purple. I took her arm. "Hong?" I asked. But she didn't respond. Instead a thin froth began to form at her lips. Glossy bubbles gathered about her mouth. They were starting to spill onto her chin. "Hong!" I said again and shook her arm. But her eyes were empty, as though she couldn't see me. And her body started to tip toward me. "Hong!" She dropped onto her side on my lap.

"Help!" I screamed. "Somebody help! Somebody help her!"

I took her by the shoulders and shook, but she only groaned.

Then someone was pulling her out of my arms. "What happened?" she asked. Another woman picked up the pot. "Did she eat the yucca skins?" I nodded, and two other women ran to the communal kitchen. "Those are poisonous," said the woman who was now cradling my big sister. I noticed the woman's black skirt and her crisp scarf, and I realized that she was a Mei Kong.

The two women returned from the kitchen with a bottle of fish sauce and some salt. They poured these into the yucca skin pot and handed it to the Mei Kong. She opened Hong's bubbly lips and poured the dark liquid into her mouth. I could hear it dribbling down her throat. She swallowed. The Mei Kong propped her up and slapped her on the back over and over. Two of the other women leaned over to rub her stomach.

Through all of this, Hong only moaned. Her face was still blank. Her eyes still empty.

And then suddenly it changed. The life came back to her eyes, a wild, fiery kind of life. She opened her mouth, and out it poured, a putrid but colorful, bubbly wash. She sputtered and coughed, and then breathed a gasping breath. Her cheeks regained their usual pinkish hue, but she still looked miserable, her mouth pursed into a wobbly frown.

"Hong," I said, and she looked at me. This time, I knew she could see me.

She vomited again.

The women were quick, they fed her another serving of the fish sauce and salt. Almost as soon as she had swallowed it, she was throwing up again.

When she was finished, she looked up at me. "It's gone," she said. "My stomach is empty."

So the Mei Kong patted her back one last time, and she and the other women wandered off.

"Come on," I said. "Let's go get cleaned up." I held out my hand to help her up. She took it, and we walked. We went to the water tanks. We splashed our faces and hands until all remnants of the vomit had been washed from our skin. Hong gurgled some water in her throat. I began to wonder if the same poison that had struck Hong, was working its way through my stomach. I tried making myself throw up, but nothing would come, and my stomach felt fine, so I concluded that there was nothing to worry about. I took a drink of water, and Hong and I walked back to her hut. We went inside this time and sat on her mat.

It was quiet inside, and we could have a conversation, just two sisters.

"You didn't know it was poisonous?" I asked. "They didn't tell you?"

Again, she shrugged. "They didn't know I was going to take it."

We were silent for a moment. And the silence stirred up all the things we had been talking about when she had gotten sick.

"Do you think he's dead?" Hong asked.

"Pa? I don't know," I said because how could I give up hope when there was a chance? Even a small chance. "Do you?"

"I don't know."

"What if he's out there, hiding in the jungle?" It was a glorious image, our father the hero, escaping the Khmer Rouge and slinking through the shadows, waiting in the darkness until it was safe to come find us.

"What if he ran away?" she said. "Or what if he's just off working at some other camp."

"I hope," I said.

"I hope, too."

"But we can't go back to Steang Chas," I told her. "We can't risk them finding us. That's why I wanted you to know where we are now. The town just west of here."

She nodded.

"I heard gun shots," I whispered.

Hong turned to me now with wide eyes.

"Just a few," I said. "But I heard them. I don't know what's going to happen, but I know this, if you hear the sound of guns, of fighting…well, fighting is good. Change is good."

Hong was still looking at me. Her eyes still wide. Her mouth open a little.

So I looked into those wide eyes, and I spoke slowly. Because this was important. "Hong, if we have to run. If we have to do something. If we have to go somewhere, we need to find each other. If something happens, look for us. Find us in the town. Just west of here."

I said this in hope. I didn't really believe it would happen. I couldn't have dared to believe it.

What Hope Sounds Like

But after I had said good bye to my big sister. And after I had walked back to the town. Even after I had settled onto my own mat beside Peou. After night had fallen black and silent. I heard it again. Gunshots. Hope.

Chapter 18

At Last We Were Five

The sound of gunshots continued. Sometimes only once every few weeks, sometimes several times in one week. They punched holes in our despair like a needle would break holes in a black sheet of paper. Each prick let a new ray of light in. Gunshots were becoming more frequent.

Then, one morning, we saw it, a great crowd of people moving like a shadow over the land. They moved slowly on foot, each carrying a great burden – a bundle of pots and pans, a bag of rice, a mat rolled up with clothes, all of their belongings. They came from the east, and slowly they trudged through our town. It reminded me of that day, so long ago, when we left Phnom Penh, the day when all this began. Never since, had I seen so great a crowd moving.

Little did I know, it was just the opposite. This slow tide of people meant that the Khmer Rouge had finally lost their grip on the city that had once been my home. The Vietnamese had taken Phnom Penh, Pol Pot had fled, and the Khmer Rouge were retreating westward. And they drove the people of Cambodia like cattle with them.

After the first crowd had passed through our village, all was quiet again. We thought one village must have been redistributed, much like our camp had been a few months before. We thought it was finished. But when we woke the next morning it happened again. Another wave of people slowly drifted through our town,

At Last We Were Five

clogged our road, passed through, and eventually were gone. It happened again the next day. Always from the east they came. Always towards the west, they trudged. It seemed the whole country of Cambodia was pouring from one side to the next, and our town was the spout.

And then one day, it was our turn. It was a day filled with commotion. "Pack up!" The Mei Kong was shouting. "Gather your things. Get your rations."

So we did as she said, but we did it slowly. Slowly I rolled up our mats. Slowly I gathered our things into a bundle.

"Are we going?" Kann asked me,

"Not yet," I told him. "We have to wait for Hong."

But already the town was beginning to empty. Everywhere, families were stepping out into the road, their belongings slung onto their backs. The Mei Kong stood in the center, giving directions, pointing down the road to the west.

There was a line of people stretching out of the communal kitchen and along the road. The people I saw coming out of the kitchen carried large bags of rice. So I gathered all three of my siblings, and we got in line. When we reached the table, the woman counted us. "One, two, three, four," and she pulled a small bag of salt and a giant sack of rice from behind the table and pushed it toward us. It was heavy, but Thy and I were able to drag it outside. Then we distributed the rice between a bucket and a few smaller bags to make it easier to carry.

"Are we going, now?" Kann asked, as we piled all of our belongings in a heap on the dirt road.

"Not without Hong," I said. "She knows where we are. She'll come."

At Last We Were Five

The crowds were getting thicker. Not only were the residents of our town spilling into the road, but a new crowd from the east was coming. "Look for Hong," I told my siblings. So Thy ran across the road and climbed onto a pile of hay. Kann stood on a tree stump on the edge of the road. I stood in the center, Peou at my side, and we peered anxiously into the crowd.

They were moving slowly, but they were thick, and many of them were taller than we were. I stepped on top of our rice bucket, which gave me an extra foot or so of height, enough to make me as tall as most of the adults coming through. I could see Kann, now, across the road. "Do you see her?" I called.

"No!" he shouted back. "You?"

"No." We strained our eyes, studying every face that passed by. When a particularly thick wad of people came through, I had to bob, moving my head around to as many different positions as I could manage, while still standing on the bucket. Even so, I could not see into the center of the crowd. When they had passed, Kann called out to me again. "I hope we didn't miss her!"

"I know," I said. I had begun to worry the same thing.

After a while, the crowd began to thin. Almost all of our town's residents were gone. Its road travelled only by feet passing through. We watched every face closely. None of them was Hong's.

"Maybe she's already ahead of us." It was Thy who called out to me this time. "Should we go?"

"Not yet," I said. I could see them in the distance. Another thick knot approaching. It seemed to be the end of the crowds coming from the east. If she wasn't there, I knew, we would have no choice but to go without her.

At Last We Were Five

Slowly the crowd approached, but when they did, it was as thick a crowd as ever. I held tightly to Peou's hand, as she stood on her little tippy toes and shaded her eyes with her hand. I studied each face carefully but quickly. One at a time, I ruled them out. *Not Hong. Not Hong. Not Hong.* I leaned to the right, turned to the left, craned my neck out, rose on my toes, did everything I could to see every head that passed by.

She was only about ten feet away, when I saw her. And the crowds between us were dense. I sprang off the rice bucket and pushed my way towards her, reaching a hand between bodies to grasp hers. She saw me then, and her mouth opened with recognition and relief. With a firm grip on my hand, she followed me to the rice bucket where Peou was waiting. Kann waved cheerfully and hopped across the road to us as soon as he found an opening. Thy came close behind.

We clasped one another in one big, many-layered hug. Another link on the chain. At last, we were five!

But we had to get going. We had waited so long already. So I pulled myself away from their familiar arms. "Come on. We need to go. This way."

And just like that, I was leading them. Even my bong. Gathering up all of our belongings, they followed me.

Chapter 19

Someone Who Would Hear Me

We started our journey, following the crowds. We were headed west like the Mei Kong had said, but as we walked there was no Mei Kong to give us orders. There were no soldiers. No one to make us go one way or another. And so as we came to crossroads, we began to turn. The crowd did it. We followed. Soon we were heading south. Then we were heading east. Toward the sound of the gunshots. Toward the sound of hope.

As we walked, we came across treasures. Cast offs from the crowds before us. Things that had been too heavy, too great a burden. We eagerly gathered up everything we could use. Some pots and pans. A bag of rice. Water bottles made of aluminum or hollowed bamboo. A sack of dried fish. Before long, it was more than we could carry. We gave the lighter things to Peou and Kann – the blankets, clothing, and bamboo bottles. Thy could carry some of the pots and pans, but that left the bags and bucket of rice, the salt, and the larger pans for Hong and me. It was too much.

So we gathered together all the rice and salt in a pile on the edge of the dirt road. "Bong Hong," I said to my older sister. "Stay here with these until I come back." Then I lifted the giant rice pot. "Come on," I said to my younger siblings, and together, the four of us trudged down the road with our burdens.

Someone Who Would Hear Me

The crowd had thinned now, but we knew where we were going. We were going east. We were going to where things might be better. After we had walked about a mile, I told my siblings to stop. They were tired, and ready for a break. They set their bags down on the side of the road and sat next to them. "I'll be back," I told them, putting the rice pot down beside them.

Then I turned around and walked back toward Hong. It was easy walking now. Weighed down by nothing but the sky. I walked with light, bouncing steps. Things were going to get better.

When I reached Hong, she was sitting quietly in the shade of a bush, all of our food gathered around her feet. The whole world seemed quiet. The crowds had gone. We were alone under a blue sky. All around us as far as the eye could see, low bushes and brush rambled. The air was still.

Hong stood when she saw me. She lifted the bucket of rice, and I balanced a bag on each of my shoulders. Together we walked back towards our siblings. Two sisters walking alone on a road.

Suddenly there was a rustling in the bushes. A flash of black cotton and rubber, the dark glint of sunlight on a gun barrel. He jumped out onto the road and raised his gun in the air.

Hong and I stumbled backward, holding our breath.

"Where are you going?" the soldier asked.

But we were too scared to breathe, how could we answer? Even if we could have found our voices, what could we say? We were going wherever the road led us. We were going where we hoped it was better. We were going to freedom. Is there a name for such a place?

Someone Who Would Hear Me

"Go that way!" the soldier snapped, waving his gun to the west.

We stood still. Silent.

"Go that way!" he said again, pointing towards the Khmer Rouge camps. Towards slavery. Towards the living dead.

There was nothing we could say. And we could not bring ourselves to move.

He raised his gun in the air and split the sky with a bullet. It was so loud, my body lurched backward. "Move! Move!"

Hong and I turned slowly. We began walking the way we had come. Away from freedom. Away from hope. Away from our brother and sisters.

We were slow, with the weight of the rice on our thin bodies. We were slower really than we needed to be. Slow because every step was a step in the wrong direction. Slow because we would need to cover this ground again. The soldier, though, walked with quick, anxious steps. His eyes roamed the horizon nervously. He ran ahead of us until his body slowly shrank with the distant road. When he was the size of my fist, he turned around and shouted at us. "If I see you two going the wrong way again, I'll shoot you!" He pointed his gun to the sky and cut another jagged wound in the sky, and then he turned and ran.

We followed along behind him for a few more steps. Just until he was fully out of sight. Then I looked at Hong. She looked at me. We turned around.

We moved quickly this time, retracing our steps. The rice was heavy, but not as heavy as the thought of Peou, Kann, and Thy, so far away, waiting. So we ran. We ran as fast as we could. Our feet hurried along, while our heads turned, looking over our shoulders, watching for a sign of the soldier. We ran until we stumbled to a halt at a fork in the road. The dusty path parted around a tree. One path wound around the bushes to the left and out of sight behind the brush. The other meandered to the right and over a hill. I didn't remember which one we'd come from.

I looked to Hong, but she wore the same blank expression I must have worn. "Which way do we go?" I asked. Hong said nothing.

I stood still a moment. Somewhere, down one of these paths, the rest of our family sat, waiting for us. Thy, Kann, and Peou. Three links in a chain. I had worked so hard to bring us together. If we went the wrong way, how long would they wait? I remembered our uncle who had met us at the train station a year before, how eagerly he had promised to return in a few hours, how we had waited patiently. I remembered how sad my father had looked when we boarded the train without him. I remembered how we had never seen him again.

I looked at the two dirt paths and tried to remember. But all I could recall was the soldier's black tire sandals. The jolting sound of his gun.

Which way do I go? Which way do I go?

There was nothing I could do. There was no way I could know.

So I did the only thing you can do when there is nothing you can do. I hoped. I hoped again there was someone somewhere who would hear me. Someone who would help. *God?* I prayed. It was a question. It was followed by another question. *Which way do I go?* And then a request. *Please. Please show me which way to go.*

Someone Who Would Hear Me

It didn't happen in my mind. It happened in my feet. They began moving to the left. So I followed them. And Hong followed me. We hurried down the path, and I hoped that we had chosen the right way.

We ran down the path. We began to see other people again. Families like ours resting with their piles of belongings. We hurried past them.

At last we rounded a bush, and there they were. Kann's body slumped with boredom. Thy's face lined with worry. Peou's lips lighting with a smile at the sight of us. I dropped the bags of rice to put my arms around them. To feel their nearness. To link us together again.

"Where have you been?" Thy cried. "We were so worried!"

"Everyone else was going," Kann said. "Passing us by."

But there was no time to talk. We had to keep moving. We had to get somewhere else. We had to get as far away as we could. "Hurry," I said, letting go to pick my rice bags up again. "Let's go."

Thy reached for the pots and pans. "No, leave it," I told her. "Take only what we can carry together." She looked at me in surprise.

"We stay together. We're not going to separate again," I told them. I said it again as I watched Peou lift her bag onto her back. "We're not going to separate. Not ever again."

Chapter 20

Enough Sunshine in Me

This time we didn't walk. We ran. As best as we could with small feet and heavy bags. Before long we heard it. Gunshots. This time, they were close. It was the sound of hope, but it was also the sound of danger. We ducked down as best as we could, hunching our backs and bending our knees. Still we ran. As long as we could.

Finally, we could run no more, could move no more. We needed rest. We stumbled to a stop at a place in the road where crowds had gathered. They, too, had stopped for a break. I sat on the ground. My feet ached with the rest almost more than they had with the running. I reached into the bag and pulled out some dried rice and dropped a handful into the palms of each of my siblings. We were silent as we ate, except for the crunch of rice and the sound of our own heavy breaths.

All around us, people were doing the same. Sitting on their sacks of rice. Eating as quickly as they could. There was a kind of safety in it, this wall of bodies around us. An old woman was walking around. She was pale-skinned and curved with age like a crescent moon, and her face glowed with a smile that seemed as ill-placed here as a moon at midday. She would stop at each cluster of people and say something in a low voice, and then she moved on. When she came to us, she crouched down in front of me.

"We're going to that tree-line over there," she said, pointing with her pale chin. "There might be some soldiers there. Don't worry. Just follow me." She smiled and stood up.

I stood too, motioning to my siblings to do the same. We gathered our bags and followed her. The crowds began moving, too, stuttering forward towards that tree-line. We moved as fast as we could. Like a herd of cows, we thundered through the field, shaking the earth with the weight of our feet. When we reached the trees, their shadows fell over us like a shield. There in the shade stood two soldiers, but they didn't wear the black cotton of the Khmer Rouge. Each wore a light green military uniform and a sun-bleached helmet on their heads. They spoke Vietnamese. Behind them stood more soldiers in a line. We pressed together to move between them, forming a narrow line. Some people pulled their hats over their foreheads or turned their faces to the ground to hide. When I reached the first soldier, he took the bags off my shoulders, and felt them with his fingers. Then he handed them back with a nod, and I shuffled forward. Beside the next soldier, the old woman was standing. She pointed at me. "This one is my daughter," she told him in Vietnamese. She pointed behind me. "That one is my son. My daughters right there." She kept pointing at children, not only my siblings but others. The soldier nodded and ushered us all through.

We kept moving until we came to a town. It was large and bustling, with hundreds of people and big, stable huts like the ones Mei Kong would had lived in. I looked everywhere, but I couldn't see any Khmer Rouge soldiers. It seemed we had reached it. Vietnamese territory. Freedom. We had escaped. We had rice, rice to last us for a while, and there was no one to make us work.

Enough Sunshine in Me

I could have danced. Even with my sore feet and my aching shoulders, I could have leapt for joy.

But there were my siblings, holding their bags and looking up at me with patient faces. They were waiting for instructions. "Come on," I said. "Let's find a place to stay."

As we walked, I listened. I could hear pieces of conversation. Cheerful voices. "The Vietnamese zone!" I heard. "Liberated!"

We found a small corner where we could lay our blankets down for the night. We lit a fire and boiled some rice. We fell asleep that night, that first night of freedom in four years.

In the morning, I woke up early. The sun was only a thin sliver of light on the horizon, just rising, but there was enough sunshine inside me to light our whole day. I was ready for this new life. This freedom.

I knew we hadn't reached true safety yet. The Khmer Rouge and the Vietnamese were still fighting. This town could be taken back any day. We had to keep moving. So I woke my brother and sisters. We moved from town to town. For weeks we travelled, looking for a place that was safe. Looking for a place where we could make our lives.

Chapter 21

What We Don't Need

After two weeks, we came to a town. It had once been a city. I could see the remnants. Buildings made of cement; walls plastered with stucco. Row houses. They were in ruins now, but I could recognize in them something familiar. Something similar to the life I had once known. Back when our family was whole. It was hot, and we looked for a place in the shade to rest, but this town was full of people like us. Everywhere I looked, I could see them, gathering on the broken patios of the houses, clustered in the thin shadows that stretched next to the cement walls. It took us a while, but at last we found a spot to put our things down. Peou gathered wood for a fire, and Kann went for some water. While Hong got ready to cook some rice, I went off to explore the town. Sometimes I could scavenge food or supplies that were abandoned by weary travelers.

As I walked, scanning the village for anything that might be helpful, I saw other people who were also scanning. They stood, much like I had a few weeks before, on overturned crates or pots, giving them height to see through the crowds, and they looked with uplifted chins and hopeful eyes. I knew those faces. They were looking for family. All throughout the town I saw them.

But then I saw something else. A crowd had gathered farther down the road. They stood in a big knotted circle, all facing inward and shouting with low, angry voices. The crowd was too thick for me to see what was inside. Because I was small, I could slip through: beneath the raised arms of a middle-aged woman, in the narrow space between two young men. I pushed my way into the front where I could see.

There in the center of the crowd knelt four Khmer Rouge soldiers. Their hands were bound behind their back and their faces hung heavy with shame. Their gaze did not leave the ground.

The whole crowd was rumbling with anger, but one woman's voice rose high above the rest. She was old and frail, but she stepped into the center and looked down at the four men with disgust. "You killed my children!" she screamed. "You made me suffer!" She leaned down to strike one of them on the head—the head, the most sacred and respected part of the body. He did not resist her but let his head swing gently with the impact. "What goes around comes around," she said, her voice lower now. "Now we will kill you slowly."

At this there was a unified cry from the whole crowd. The woman took a slow step to the next man. "You deserve it," she hissed, and knocked him on the head with her knuckles. "You had no mercy on *us*," she said to the next. This time she spat on him before she struck his head. "I have no one left." When she had struck all four, she stepped back into the masses, and the crowd surged with an angry howl. Then another woman stepped forward. She was younger and she held a rock in her hands. She didn't say anything, but her face was red and pinched with the fierceness of her anger. She smashed the rock into the faces of each of the men, and with each hit, the crowd roared. Then a man stepped forward. He was tall and very thin. He spat on them first. While the saliva dribbled down their faces, he kicked them. One by one. "You killed them!" he shouted. "Innocent people!"

What We Don't Need

All this time, the four men said nothing. They did not raise their voices to defend themselves. Nor did they lift their eyes or brace themselves for the strikes. They only hung their heads in shame. It was like they knew how wrong they were. It was like they had known all along.

Then someone found a bamboo switch. He carried it through the crowd and looked at the four men, his face pursed, sorrow twisted to fury. Then with a snap he cracked it down onto their backs. I leapt back, lest the arc catch me by accident. Then I took another step, pressing deeper into the crowd. Then another step, even though I knew I was out of reach. Farther and farther back I went until I couldn't see them anymore. Until I broke free from the bodies. Until I was surrounded by fresh air. Until I was alone on the street.

I did not know those men. I didn't know what they had done or whom they had killed. If they had killed my father, I didn't know. If they had killed that woman's children or that man's wife I didn't know. I didn't know why they had joined the Khmer Rouge. I didn't know what led them to the choice that they had made. Maybe they had been following orders. Maybe they had had no choice. How could I know? How could I judge them? There was a kind of sorrow that hung over me now. A heavy gray weight when I thought of those four men and the shame that pulled their faces to the ground. The fact that they did not resist their fate. There was a kind of healing in that.

What if they were the ones...? I thought to myself. *What if they were the ones who killed Pa?* But even so, I felt nothing. I felt no need to push back into the crowd. I felt no desire to add my fists to those that had already struck them. *If they killed Pa,* I thought as the crowd before me roared, *I don't need to do anything. What good would it do?*

There was a kind of freedom in that.

I turned and walked back. My siblings were waiting. The rice was probably ready. But still this sadness hung over me. *I don't need it.* I couldn't shake these words from my mind. *We don't need it. There's no need. What does it accomplish?*

I sat down next to Hong, and she put a bowl of hot rice in my hands. I ate it quietly. I was grateful for my sisters and my brother who sat beside me. I was grateful for those of us who had made it through and had made it together.

I thought of the sorrow of the old woman who had screamed. I remembered the fury in the lines of her face. Lines that had been riverbeds of tears. Tears for each child. One after another. I didn't know what had happened to her children. I didn't know, when she saw those four men, what she saw. How could I know? How could I judge her?

Still, her cries echoed in my mind. The rumbling of the crowd. The guilt-hung faces of the men. These things would not leave me.

We don't need it, I thought. *We don't need revenge.*

Chapter 22

There He Is Again

The next town we came to was another crowded one, bustling with partial families like ours. Broken and looking for the missing pieces. Each one was scrambling to find something stable. A way to make a living in this strange new world without communal kitchens. Something to do in this silence, this absence of a Mei Kong barking orders every morning. A place to fall asleep at night and to wake up in the morning. A reason to get up when you woke.

We were looking for these things, too. And we were on our own. No grownups to take charge. No one who knew anything about finding a job or a home. It was up to us. It was up to me.

A cluster of siblings, clutching our bags, we explored the town, peering through crowds to see this new place. But there were too many people around us. They eclipsed our view of our surroundings. Then we rounded a corner.

That was when we first saw the temple.

It rose up, above the heads of the crowd, above the thatched roofs of the bamboo huts, above the chattering noise and the squawking of roosters. I could see its roof first, clay red tiles in an arc against the blue sky. And then, as we came closer, we saw the colors painted across the edge of the roof, brilliant pictures in oranges and yellows. Beneath them, the white pillars rose, tall and slender with golden figures perched at the top. It was the first time we'd seen color since we'd drowned our own clothes in black dye.

The temple was no longer a place of worship. On that day it was a market place. Swarming with people who held out in their palms objects for trade. Food, rice, fish, rubber shoes - things that we needed - for gold or jewels –things that we didn't have. Even so, as I stepped onto its white and blue tiles, I couldn't help but do so with awe and reverence. It had been so long since I'd been captured by beauty.

Once inside, I looked up. The paint was cracked and peeling, and water stains dribbled down from holes in the roof, but you could still see it. Beautiful images painted on the ceiling, pictures of a village, candles lit and incense burning, prayers rising into the sky. The people in these paintings were more alive than the people I had seen every day for the last four years. They lived on an earth full of color and beauty. And there was heaven, shining down in golden clouds, and the people kneeling before God as he reached his hands forward to bless them. *Wow.* Even in my thoughts, it was a whisper. *There He is again. There is God.* The only God I had ever known. For so long we had pretended He didn't exist. Had been too afraid to say His name, even in a whisper. The Khmer Rouge did not allow a god. For so long He had been invisible. But now that I could see Him again, I knew that He had been there all along.

Down here, on these tiles upon which my feet stood, the temple was as busy as the road had been. It was not only a marketplace but also temporary housing for all who needed it. And we did. So we found an empty spot and set down our belongings. This would be our home for a little while.

There He Is Again

While we were settling in, I began to see pieces coming back together.

There was a statue of Buddha which had been torn down and broken, but someone had reassembled the pieces as best as they could. Of course, it didn't stand right, and the stones no longer formed the right shape. But I could see it for what it had been. I could see it for what it represented.

Sometimes people would come to kneel before the statue. They would light incense, if they had it, and once again prayers would rise in a frail line of smoke. I would watch their lips move in prayer "Which way should I go?" they would ask. "Direct me. Where do I go to find my family? Show me the way." Over and over again, their mouths would form the words. And the words would rise with the smoke.

The sight stirred something in Hong. It had been so long. So she took me by the hand. "Let's go," she said, and led me to the statue. We waited our turn and then knelt side by side. I don't know what Hong prayed as we sat there in silence, but I prayed a question. *What should we do?* I asked it over and over.

The temple was our home now, and we quickly settled into a routine. Kann and Thy went off every day to find fire wood. Hong would build the fire and cook our rice. Peou always stayed in our spot to watch our belongings. I spent my first day walking around the temple, watching the buyers and sellers, and thinking. We had plenty of rice for now, but it would not last forever. We had to find a way to get more. We had to find a way to make a living. But as I watched the hands that exchanged goods back and forth under the temple ceiling, I saw that none of the things people wanted to

There He Is Again

trade for were things that we had. Many of them traded in gold. They held out long chains of golden links, chains just like the ones my father used to make. They would count the links, cut it, then hand over the severed gold. But we had no gold. What could we do?

And then I noticed something. Something that I saw in nearly every exchange—as the woman wrapped up a fish for a sale, as the child gathered up the rice balls she'd purchased, as the man scooped a spoonful of pickled fish—all of these traders needed something to package their goods. They used whatever they could find: a torn piece of paper, a corn husk, a leaf. I noticed that many used banana leaves, whose surfaces were wide and smooth and flexible. There had to be banana trees nearby. Yes, this was it. I had found our commodity.

The next day I went looking for banana trees. They weren't hard to find. There was a whole orchard nearby thick with trees that were green and rich with so many giant papery leaves. I stood on my tiptoes to pull the first branch down, peeling it away from the tree as far as I could with my own strength. Then, with a machete, I cut the stem from the trunk. Leaf after leaf, I harvested them, until I had a giant pile beside me. Then I sat in the shade of the leaves that remained, and with the machete, I sliced down the center of each leaf, separating the crisp green paper from the thick center stem. I discarded the stems and folded the cut leaves into neat little rectangles. When I was finished, I gathered these into a stack, and carried them home.

Even banana leaves are heavy when you gather up a hundred of them, and my walk back to the temple was slow. When I arrived and showed the first merchant my wares, he was very interested and gave me a handful of salt for a stack of my banana leaves. I moved through

There He Is Again

the temple, offering leaves to all the sellers. Before long, my leaves were gone, and I had enough resources to trade for a bag of rice. "Tomorrow," I told Hong, as she scooped a cup of rice to pour into our pot. "You're coming with me to the banana trees."

The rainy season came to our town. There were no walls to the temple, only columns to hold up the roof. But our family's spot was deep inside the temple, and there were many other families between us and the outside. Their bodies blocked most of the wind. But the rain still slipped in through the chips in the temple roof. It plunged down in glittering threads that pooled in puddles like folds of silk on the tile around us. We arranged our bodies between the leaks, and we set out pots and bowls to capture the water where it fell.

Then we lay down on our backs and looked up at the painted ceiling above. Beneath the vibrant pictures, a ribbon of golden words trailed along the edge of the ceiling. A swirling and curling script against a brilliant blue, these characters were almost as beautiful as the pictures themselves. They were letters we recognized, as if from another world. One in which we had gone to school and read books. But it had been so long since we'd even admitted we were literate, let alone had something to read. We tried the sounds out slowly, shaping them with our tongues. They were strange and mystical sounds, not the words that we spoke every day. This was Sanskrit, the ancient language, whose meaning we didn't know. Still, it seemed too beautiful not to try to unravel it in our minds, not to unspool it from our mouths, this reminder that there was something more. Something beyond rice and work and sleep.

There He Is Again

The people in the temple were nomads like us. New ones came every day and old ones left. Always looking for something, someone. One day, we found an open space on the tiles next to us. A place that was free of leaks.

"Let's move there!" Thy cried, pointing to the bare tiles. "Next to Eang!"

Eang was a little girl Thy's age. I often saw them playing together when I returned from my banana leaf harvest. She had a little brother Kann's age, and the boys often played as well.

So we slid all of our belongings over and settled into a new spot under the temple ceiling.

In the evenings, we would watch Eang's mother cook food for her two children. At night, they would lay down on their mats, and she would sit beside them and sing lullabies until they fell asleep. And between the lullabies, she would lean over them and whisper the words every child longs to hear. "Shh. Don't be afraid. I'm here." Something was familiar about it. Nostalgic. It reminded us what we were missing. It stirred a longing that we had forgotten the name for.

There was a moment when I sat quietly, my back against the temple column, and I watched as she sang. As I watched, tears rained down. They dripped down my cheeks, onto my chest, down to my lap. *It's not going to happen,* I thought, as the tears fell. *It's not going to happen to me.*

This was what mothers did. Cared for their sons and daughters. It was who mothers were. And I didn't have one. Peou, Kann, Thy, and Hong were asleep on the cool tiles. I lay down next to them. *I don't have one,* I thought, as the tears on my cheeks formed a sticky film

There He Is Again

between my skin and the mat. *But I must be one.* I cried myself to sleep that night. The loss felt too great. Unbearable. But then day came. I woke up and rose to gather more banana leaves. It was true that I no longer had a mother. It was true that I never would again. But there was work to be done. I had to move on.

Each day, Hong and I went to harvest our banana leaves, and each day we sold them for rice, salt, and dried fish. At last, we had a sense that we could keep this going. But now that we had it, it wasn't enough. To have a stomach full of rice. To hold back the hunger. It wasn't quite enough. I began to crave more than just food. More than just filling the emptiness. I remembered what it was like to taste. To hold something in your mouth that more than filled it. Something delicious.

I had seen women in the market place selling balls of rice. I had watched carefully as they made them. First, they cooked the rice. Then they let it cool to a gentle warmth. Then they sprinkled yeast into the pot and rolled the rice between their palms until it formed balls like giant pearls. They set these treasures in a bowl and then wrapped them with layer upon layer. Towels, clothes, whatever was on hand, tight enough to block out the fresh air. They left this bundle to ferment for two days, and when those two days had passed, they would unwrap the layers. The first thing to break through was the smell, fragrant and sweet. Then I would peer over their shoulders to look inside. The balls sat, as glossy and shiny as any real pearl, in a pool of glittering wine. I decided I could do this. So with my next stack of banana leaves, I bought some yeast. I carried it home to cook the rice.

There He Is Again

Eang's mom, who was sitting not far away with her own pot of rice, smiled at me as I worked. It was nice, the smile. It was the same good feeling that I got when I watched Thy playing with Eang on the edge of the temple. When I saw Kann and Eang's brother laughing together. Friendship.

We were rediscovering things we had forgotten about. Things we had missed so long we had forgotten that we missed them.

One day as we cooked, Hong and I told Eang's mom about how we had come here. We told her about our family, about our mother and brother who had died, and our father who probably had. And she told us about hers, how her husband had fallen ill and how they had taken him to the hospital, but he had died. Just a month later, Eang had gotten sick, so very sick. She told me how she had brought her daughter, tiny and frail, to the same hospital. She had laid her daughter down, worried, hopeful that they could help the child live. But a nurse had leaned forward and whispered. "Take your daughter away from here," she had said. "If your daughter stays here, she will die." There was more than despair in the woman's low voice. It was a warning. Eang's mom had thought of her husband, of how they'd brought him here. Of how he had died the next day. And she began to wonder. So she took her daughter home, and nursed her herself. Eang had survived. Eang's mom told me what she had later heard, how at the hospital, the nurses had injected something into the patient's veins to kill them quickly, to rid themselves of the burden.

Eang's family had a story that was sad like ours. But they were here. They had survived. Like us.

Two days later, the rice wine balls were ready. They were just like the ones I had seen, floating in a pool

There He Is Again

of their own syrup. I scooped one up with a spoon and slid it into my mouth.

Oh! the things I had forgotten. Sweetness. Rich, sugary juice dribbling down my chin. Slurping the wine. Licking my lips. Licking the spoon. Reaching into the pot for more.

I decided I would make these every day.

So my days were filled with banana leaves and rice wine balls. My siblings ate them as eagerly as I did. And next to us, sat our friends, who smiled and laughed. Friends.

Chapter 23

The Answer to the Question

We lived there at the temple for a few months. We harvested and sold banana leaves. We made rice wine balls and remembered the taste of sweetness. The children played with Eang and her brother. And at night, we lay down beneath paintings of heaven. We had found a life here, a means of providing for ourselves, a living. But I could not stop wondering about the next day. I could not stop thinking about the future. How long would we stay here? Where were we? So I began to listen as I walked through the market place, trading banana leaves, as we huddled by our fire at night, everywhere that I could hear grownup voices. I listened for names of towns. I listened for directions. I listened for words like "north" or "south" or "miles". I listened for numbers. Slowly I gathered the pieces.

We were in Battambang province. It was about 150 miles to Phnom Penh, the city where I had been born. Where Chun had ridden his bicycle across the roof tops, my arms wrapped around his waist. It was the city where Chao's laughter had bubbled out, as he sat in my lap and we soared along on that thin line between the city and the sky and he cried "Go faster! Go faster!" That place was still there, somehow, 150 miles to the southeast.

A part of me wanted to believe it was home, that we could return, that if we went back, my brothers would

The Answer to the Question

be there, that somehow pieces of our family could be restored. But the rest of me knew that the city was empty, empty at least of everything I wanted. Even if our building still stood. Even if our apartment was still there, still clean, still full of the books and clothes and beautiful comforts I had longed for in the early days of the Khmer Rouge. Even if the steps still led up to the roof and a clear night sky, to a moon so full and so close you could reach out to touch it. Even so, Chao would not be there, standing in the doorway with his smile wide and his dimples pressed into each cheek. My mother would not be leaning over the soup pot, her face awash in steam. My father would not be sitting on the roof with his harmonica, flinging his song into the night. It would be empty.

I considered the more practical hopes. That we might find my uncle or my grandmother in Phnom Penh. That if Chun or my father were alive, the city might be the first place they would look for us. But I also weighed the more practical concerns. The Vietnamese had taken over all of Cambodia now, had forced the Khmer Rouge into hidden pockets in the jungle, but I knew now how fickle war was, and how easily she changed allegiances. Any day, it seemed, the tides could change. The Khmer Rouge could come crashing back through our country, could return to Phnom Penh, could retake any village or city in Cambodia. No, we were not safe in this country.

So I considered making the trek to Vietnam. We had heard of those who had fled across its borders for refuge. But I wondered about these Vietnamese. No, they were not brutal and blood thirsty as the Khmer Rouge had been, but these soldiers, there was something about them – with their guns and their green uniforms – something that I didn't trust. They were communist, too,

The Answer to the Question

and who was to say that they wouldn't turn on us as our own people had?

No. We had to get away. Far away.

It was only 50 miles to the Thai border. 50 miles West. The journey to Thailand was short but more dangerous. I had heard of the dangers of the jungle that bridged the two countries. It was full of all the usual hazards of any jungle: elephants, bears, snakes, and spiders. But there were also the dangers that the war had brought. Land mines were woven into the earth to stop smugglers and escapees such as us. Worse, the Khmer Rouge, the very enemy from which we were fleeing had fled to these jungles themselves. They were hiding there now, desperate and famished. In the jungle they still had their guns and their cruelty. And we, we had nothing to defend ourselves.

What's more, the Vietnamese would not willingly relinquish the people they had bought with their own bullets and blood. If they found us trying to slip away from their liberation, they would surely use the same force they had used against the Khmer Rouge. A trip across the Thai border would have to be a secret one.

It was a hard decision. One that would determine everything.

Which way do we go? Which way? The words ran through my head over and over again, even as they had when Hong and I had stood at the fork in the road. *Which way do we go?* On that day, I had raised the question to God. At the time I hadn't even been sure He was there. He had been invisible for so long. I had only hoped. And in my hope, I had asked Him, *Which way do we go?* And He had answered. He had put the way in my feet, and it had led me to my brother and sisters.

So I took my question to God.

The Answer to the Question

I went back to the broken statue. I had no incense to light, so my prayers were invisible. I knelt, and I asked Him. *Where should we go? Please show us the way. Please show us the way.*

One day, Hong and I went to the banana grove. We were pulling down leaves as we always did, peeling them from the tree, cutting their stems with the machete, talking as we worked. Suddenly I heard the *tssht tssht* sound of rustling leaves. It was like the wind but faster and more rhythmic. I had heard that sound before in the corn fields the day the spy boys had found me. It struck terror into my heart as it had that day. I looked up and saw two figures running at us through the banana trees. "Hey!" their shout sliced through the groves. I could see now that it was a man and woman, and they each held something high in the air as they ran. "Get out of here!" the man yelled. "This is our farm!"

I looked to Hong in confusion. Our farm? How could it be their farm? No one owned any land here. Not since the Khmer Rouge. But they were getting closer, and the man was still shouting. We could see what they held in their hands now. Curves of metal. Machetes. The man waved his as he ran. "What do we do?" I asked Hong. "What do we do without banana leaves?" But her eyes were wide with fear.

The man was only a few trees away now. "I'll kill you!" he screamed as he waved the machete.

We dropped the leaves we held, grabbed our bags and ran. Away from the banana trees. Away from our business. Away from stability. "If you come back I'll kill you!" He shouted after us. I could hear his voice as I ran. I could hear it long after we were out of earshot.

The Answer to the Question

We were quiet that afternoon, as we sat together around the rice pot. Even the rice wine balls didn't taste as good. Not without knowing how we'd ever get more again.

Over the next few days, I looked for more banana trees. There were a couple of other groves. They were farther away, which meant more time walking and less time gathering leaves. But each time I arrived; I found a family settled at the farm. Each time they insisted firmly that the trees were theirs and that they would not tolerate trespassing.

I walked back to the temple slowly; my head hung low and my feet were heavy. *What do we do?*

When I reached the temple, I knelt before the statue and posed the question again. *What do we do?*

I lay on my mat that night, waiting for sleep. The moon was bright and cast a yellow gleam on the temple tiles. I remembered the old woman from the rice fields that day, so long ago. "Why are you alive?" she had demanded. "Why are you alive?"

I thought back to my many brushes with death. The dysentery. The malaria. The road to the train station when I had been paralyzed. The near drowning in the river. The land mine that had taken Ny but left me. The spy boys who had left me in the corn fields.

Why are you alive? I asked myself the question. *Why?* It didn't make sense. There were too many times. *Why didn't they see Peou when we brought her to the camp? Why didn't they take us away as they had the other children?* Then I turned the question away from me. I directed it up towards the ceiling and its beautiful colors. I couldn't see them in the dark, but I knew they were there. *Why am I alive?* I asked. *Why did I choose the right way at the fork in the path? Why am I alive?*

The Answer to the Question

An answer began to form in my mind. It came in pieces, like something broken put back together carefully. It didn't fit together quite right, but still I could see it. I knew what it was.

There was someone watching us. Someone taking care of us. Every time I had asked for help there was someone who heard. Every time I had asked for help, help had come.

God, are You taking care of us? It was a frightening question to ask, too big to understand, too big to accept. But I could feel the answer washing over me with the moonlight. I could feel it seeping in.

And because of the answer, I knew what we needed to do. I knew that no risk was too great. I knew that we would make it.

The next day we were eating our midday meal of rice wine balls. The day was at its busiest. The chatter of the market filled the air, and all around us were the sounds of life and conversation. It was just the sort of setting that made private conversations safe. Beneath the noise, I heard a whisper in my ear. "Sida!" It was Eang's mom. She beckoned for Hong and me to follow her.

We rose and went to sit beside her rice pot. She spoke to us in a low voice. A voice the Vietnamese soldiers would not hear. A voice that no neighbor or passerby might listen to and repeat for community gossip. "Tomorrow we're moving," she said. "Going to another town. Going *West*. You understand." We did. I nodded.

But Hong gasped and shook her head. "It's risky!" she whispered.

"It is risky," Eang's mom echoed. "If you want," she said. "You can come." She pointed to all my

The Answer to the Question

siblings who still sat gathered around our pot, watching us with curiosity.

Hong and I rose and went back to our family. "It's too risky," Hong whispered in my ear. But she didn't know what I knew. She didn't know what I had already decided.

"What will we do if we stay?" I asked her. "If we can't sell banana leaves, what will we do?" I looked around me at the faces of my siblings. I asked her one more question. "Why would we stay?"

I brought it up to Hong a few more times that day. While we were filling our bucket with water. While we were rolling rice balls. As we lay down on our mats after the children had gone to sleep. "It's our best option, Hong," I would tell her. She would only shake her head.

The next day, as we sat down to our midday meal, I announced my decision to the family. "We're leaving with Eang's mom tomorrow," I whispered.

"No, we're not," Hong said. "It's too risky. We could be killed. Raped. Who knows? It's too dangerous, crossing the border."

I scooped up a rice ball and slid it into my mouth. We had to keep up the pretense of a normal meal in case anyone was watching. "I'm leaving with Eang's mom tomorrow," I said, and slurped the wine from the spoon. "We're going to cross the border into Thailand and find a way out of here." I licked my lips and dipped the spoon in for another rice ball. "Hong's right that it's dangerous, but there's nothing for us here." My lips closed around another rice ball. I savored its sweetness a moment and then swallowed. "This is no life." I put the spoon down and looked at my little siblings then. "Who's coming with me?"

Peou didn't hesitate. "I'll go with you, Sida."

The Answer to the Question

"Me, too," said Kann.

"I'll come," said Thy.

I picked the spoon up again and slid it under another rice ball. "Hong?" I asked. "Are you coming?"

Hong said nothing. She ate her own rice ball slowly and delicately. Even so, I could see that her chin was quivering.

She said nothing to me that night, but in the morning, as I began to pack our bags, she helped me. Then, rolling up the children's mats, she leaned forward and whispered, "I'm coming with you."

Chapter 24

A Girl Who Had Escaped Again

Before we left, we had to sell anything we couldn't carry. We dragged our bag of rice to the market and exchanged it for some gold leaves. We traded our pots and pans for a couple of golden chain links. Then I sewed the gold onto the inside of my shirt just where the waist band of my pants would hold it secure against my body. When I did this, I gave Hong the ruby and pearls that I'd carried ever since I'd found them in my father's hut. These Hong sewed into a tiny pocket inside her shirt.

We gathered up our light bags and set out from the temple and its painted ceilings. I wasn't worried. I felt certain now that this was not the last place of beauty I would see.

We spent a few weeks travelling from town to town. At last, we reached Serei Saophoan, a town less than 20 miles from the border. It was so close to Thailand that we could smell it. The market in the center of town was full of the scent of newness and rubber, fresh out of a factory, still packaged in plastic. Cambodia hadn't seen or smelled such things in four long years. We watched the men come in on their bicycles, worn and sweaty, their feet caked in mud. Then they would unload their goods in the market place. Flipflops, clean and sharp, stacks and stacks of them. Sarongs of every color, beautifully woven and crisply folded. Hats and scarves,

The Girl Who Had Escaped Again

their colors still bright. Bags of sugar. And candies. Handfuls and handfuls of them, wrapped in glossy plastic that crinkled when you touched them - just like the ones I used to trick Chun into giving me. The men would sell these goodies to a clamoring crowd. I would watch them tuck gold into their pockets with every exchange, and I noticed their smiles as they did so. Before long, their goods would be gone, and they would get on their bicycles and ride away. They'd be back a few days later with even more goods.

It didn't take much to figure out where all these delights came from, nor how much profit these smugglers must make from their trips back and forth across the Thai border and how much danger they had faced to make it.

There were no empty huts to settle into at Serei Saophoan, so we found a bench on the edge of the market and made that our home. We hoped our stay here would be short. Soon we would leave Serei Saophoan. Soon we would leave Cambodia all together. Any day now.

Eang's mom introduced us to the man who was leading the trip. He peered down at us, a tangle of five children on a bench. He eyed Peou with a worried brow. "She won't cry, will she?"

"No, she doesn't cry." I assured him.

But the worry did not leave his face. "We can't take small children," he said. "If they cry, they'll give us all away."

"She won't cry." Eang's mom said it with such firm confidence that the man gave a gentle nod.

"We'll leave soon," he told us. "Be ready. We'll let you know when it's time."

The monsoon rains came. We huddled together on our bench, five children in the rain. We had a plastic

The Girl Who Had Escaped Again

tarp, but it wasn't big enough to cover the whole bench, so we pulled it over ourselves like a blanket. It kept at least part of our bodies dry.

Each day we woke, hoping to receive word that it was time, but each day we heard nothing. And each day we watched the smugglers spread their colorful goods, fresh from Thailand, across their tables in the market place. We watched them gather fat wads of profits into their pockets. Each day I watched as our rice slowly dwindled, until there was nothing left but the smooth bottom of the bucket.

What will we eat now? I asked myself, but I had no answer with which to reply. I patted the hem of my shirt. Inside, I knew, thin sheets of gold still hid. I could break the thread, peel open the cloth, and slip one out. It could buy us enough food for a few more days. *But then what?* I asked myself, and again I did not reply. We had no idea how long we would be here. We had already stayed far longer than I had hoped. There was no telling when the group would be ready to leave. If we started spending our limited treasures now, they would soon be gone. *How can we earn a living?* It was back to that question. But we had nothing to offer for sale in the market. No banana-leaf groves nearby. Here, the market traded in machine-made products, goods from another world, a world outside Cambodia, a world on the other side of those trees. A world so close, but how long would it be until we went there?

And that was how I came upon our next plan. It was the only real source of income here. The only thing to trade. I had to be able to do it.

"We've been waiting a long time," I told Hong that night. "And I've been thinking. What if I went across the border with some of the other smugglers, and brought back something of value to sell? It would be enough to buy us food for a while. Maybe even enough for the trip. Something for security, you know?"

"All right," Hong said.

So the next day, I left, my gold leaves and chain still safely stitched into my shirt. I left Hong with the ruby and pearls. She kept these, just in case anything should happen to me.

It was day break, the sun just a blush on the fringe of the sky. A small crowd was gathering on the edge of town. I knew they were smugglers by the empty bags that some of them carried. I hovered near the edge of them until I could identify the leader. He was a young man, probably a few years older than Chun, but strong and fit. "I'm going to follow you," I told him, my voice timid – because he was my elder - and yet firm - because I wasn't going to change my mind.

He looked down at me. "If you don't keep up, you will be left behind."

"Okay," I said, but he had already walked away.

Then the group began to move into the forest. I followed, moving as quickly as I could. The hurried scramble up the path reminded me of the journey, three years before when my father had carried my limp body along the road until I was strong enough to walk. *I have no father to carry me this time. No Chun to come from behind and save me*, I told myself. *If I fall behind, I will get lost.*

The trees were large and sturdy. Their trunks were wide enough for a grown man to hide behind, and they wore a heavy, dark, bark-like armor. Each one stretched a hundred feet in the air before it spread its first branch, but from there they covered the sky in a thick mat of leaves so that no sliver of blue shone through.

The Girl Who Had Escaped Again

These leaves not only shut out the sky but also the light and the breeze, so that the air we were left to breathe was thick and heavy. But for all that the trees shut out the morning light and air, they also shut out Cambodia and the worries that come with openness and visibility. I could almost imagine myself safe.

It was a narrow path, and we walked single file. Often travelers would come down the path going the other direction, and we would squeeze to the left side of the path so that they could pass on the right. I always watched them as they went by, loaded with goods. Some on bicycles, some with a pole balanced over their shoulders, a bag hanging from each end, some on foot. I saw that many struggled under the weight of sugar bags and other heavy packages. One man came along with a huge stack of rubber flipflops on his back. They were bulky, and it was difficult to maneuver around him on the narrow path, but I could tell that they did not press into his shoulders or weary his gait as so many of the other burdens had. *That's what I'll get*, I told myself. *Flip-flops. They're light.*

We stopped at about midday – or at least the people immediately in front of me stopped. I could not see beyond them through the thick trees. So I sat down, my breath heaving to flood my lungs with as much of the cumbersome air as it could in this absence of movement. I pulled out the salted rice and fish that I had packed, unfolded it from its makeshift envelope of leaves and ate as quickly as I could. It was only a few minutes before the others were standing up again, so I crammed the last bite of rice into my mouth and stood. If I did not keep up, I would be left behind. Again, we hurried forward.

After a while, we came across a man who lay in the path grasping his ankle. We slowed our pace around

The Girl Who Had Escaped Again

him. He was part of our group. Two other men stood leaning over him. "I think it's broken," one of them said.

"What do we do?" the other asked.

I wanted to linger to find out. What would happen to the man? Would someone carry him back? But the others in front of me kept moving. Someone pushed around me from behind.

I have to keep moving, I told myself. *Or I will be left behind.*

So I scampered up the path to catch up. I never found out what happened to the man with the broken ankle.

It wasn't until dusk that the trees parted, and we came out into open land, the sky purple and dim behind. There was a market there, a few sellers with their tarps spread out. But it was late, and most of them were packing up what was left of their wares, their tarps nearly bare now in the glow of the setting sun. There was so little left. I hurried to buy what I could. First, I had to trade my gold leaves for Thai baht, colorful pieces of paper printed with numbers on them. It had been so long since I had handled real money. By the time I was done, there was only one seller who had flipflops left, and he only had two bags of the sandals to sell - the least popular sizes, I suspected - but I had to buy something. "How much?" I asked. I quickly paid for them and he handed them to me. Two dozen sandals.

It had been four years since I'd worn shoes, and I was giddy with the sudden realization that I now could. With fumbling fingers, I opened the bag with the smallest ones and pulled out the first pair. They were far too big for my feet, but with my toes squeezed tight, I could keep them on. It was a luxurious feeling, smooth rubber under your feet. A thick barrier between my skin and the ground. I relished it for a moment, taking slow steps on their gentle surface. But when I looked up, I saw the merchants packing up and remembered the urgency.

I looked around, frantic. The products were fast disappearing into the seller's bags. I saw sarongs, delicate and sparkling fabrics that I knew I couldn't afford. I looked at the bills still in my hand. When I saw a merchant with four bags of colorful hard candies still out on his tarp, I quickly traded for them. They were beautiful: bright balls of color wrapped in slick clear plastic. When I picked them up to put them in my bag, they crinkled deliciously just like they had when Chun had handed me a handful of them back home. They had been a form of currency for me as a child, and here they were again. My stomach growled as I pushed the last one into my bag. It had been a long day of walking with only a little rice and fish to eat. *Maybe I'll eat some of these candies on my way home*, I thought to myself with a smile. I had one colorful bill left in my hand, so I looked around. I was beginning to panic. Dark was settling over the market, and the last seller was packing up. In the growing darkness, I could see the smugglers heading back into the forest. But I could still carry more. I had to get everything I could from this trip. I saw a bag of sugar that he hadn't yet put away. I thrust my money forward and grabbed the bag.

I had to tie the two bags of flipflops together in a knot so that I could fling them over my shoulder. One bag hung in front of me and the other against my back. I heaved the other bag, full of sugar and candies over my other shoulder, and then hurried after the other smugglers.

The Girl Who Had Escaped Again

Darkness sank over the forest. Still, I followed the feet in front of me. The sandals on my feet sank into the mud with each step, and with each step, the mud refused to relinquish them. I had to give each foot a mighty tug, and then my foot would slip right out leaving the shoe behind. *This isn't going to work,* I muttered. I pulled the sandals out of the mud, wiped them on the trunk of a nearby tree, and then tucked them into my bag. Bare feet would just have to do.

We walked on in the growing darkness. My legs ached and my mind swirled like the leaves in a night breeze. But there was no time for stopping, no time for rest. If I didn't keep up, I would be left behind. So I stumbled along, watching only my feet and those ahead of me. In the darkness and fatigue, I wasn't paying attention. I didn't notice that this path was different, that it wasn't the way we had come

It was when I stepped out onto a wide dirt road that I knew that something was wrong. It wasn't safe to travel on the roads. Surely the soldiers would see us. But I didn't know the way home by myself. I had no choice but to follow the group. Finally, we came to a stop at a tall wooden house, grand with its thick front columns and shingled roof, and I heard the bark of Vietnamese soldiers.

There were at least a hundred of us, far more than my original group. We all sat down in rows on the flat dirt and waited quietly. I leaned towards the woman next to me. "What's going on?"

"We've been caught," she whispered back. The last of the smugglers were being ushered to their seats next to us. The soldiers must have been gathering us from all over the forest and herding us all here.

The Girl Who Had Escaped Again

Two electric lights lit the balcony of the house. Everything else lay shrouded in darkness. I thought of the treasure that I carried on my back and shoulders. I had traded all my gold for this. If they took it from me, I would have nothing to bring back. What would we eat then? I had to hide it.

Quickly, I swung the bag into my lap and opened the packages of candy. As quietly as I could manage, I stuffed them into my shirt, into my pockets, anywhere I could fit them. When my shirt could hold no more, I unrolled the cuff of my pants, tucked them into the folds, and rolled them back up. I still had two bags of candy left exposed. There was nowhere else I could hide it. I was certain that they would take the rest. There was nothing else I could do. I unwrapped one candy and popped it in my mouth. It was sweet and juicy, everything I remembered it to be. But there was no time to savor its taste. I was unwrapping the candies as fast I could and dropping them as fast into my mouth until my mouth was full and could hold no more. If these hard-won treasures were going to be confiscated, I wanted to eat as many as I could first. Sucking on them wasn't fast enough. I crunched down with my teeth and chewed their shards. They were dissolving into a thick and syrupy juice in my mouth. I swallowed and crammed more in.

Then a man stepped into the glaring light on that balcony. He was a soldier in the crisp green uniform that the Vietnamese always wore. He held a megaphone to his mouth, and his voice broke out over the crowd, crackling but loud. "Brothers and sisters!" It was our language that he spoke, but his accent was Vietnamese. "When we tell you not to go into Thailand, it's for your own safety. There are Khmer Rouge still hiding in the

The Girl Who Had Escaped Again

jungle. You could be captured or killed. We are trying to protect you. You should not be here in the jungle, doing what you're not allowed to do. We're trying to protect you."

He lowered the megaphone, and silence floated down over us, like paper drifting in the cool air. We waited there under the stillness. Minutes passed. At last the dry crackle of the megaphone snapped the silence and our breath away. "Brothers and sisters," he called out again. "We forgive you this time. Next time we catch you, we will not let you go."

There was a stirring now, as we looked around at one another. They "forgave" us? Had we misunderstood him. We looked for confirmation in each other's faces, but only found the same astonishment we felt.

"Listen," the voice crackled. "For your own safety. Don't come back into the jungle again."

We were still looking around, puzzled, trying to figure out what the man with the megaphone could mean.

"Okay brothers and sisters, you can leave."

At this, there was a sudden murmuring – a cacophony of both wondering voices and movement – the gathering of bags, the rustle of fabric as people stood. And then the sound of hurrying feet.

I joined them, gathering my bags as quickly as I could and running, candy-stuffed shirt and all, after the crowd.

It was a few hours past dawn when I reached the market at Sway Siphon. I found our park bench. Thy, Kann, and Peou were all asleep, but Hong rose to greet me. I handed her the bags – candy, flip-flops, and sugar. I didn't speak a word to her but laid down on the bench and slept. I slept with the safety of a girl who is home. A girl who had escaped danger. Again.

Chapter 25

Never Again

When I woke, it was late afternoon, and Hong had already sold all the flipflops, the candy, and the sugar. The flipflops, she told me, someone had bought from her before she even made it to the market. And the candy and sugar she had sold as soon as she had arrived. I worried then, that she had sold them too quickly and for too little, but when she showed me the pile of baht, much thicker than the one I'd held in my hand in the Thai market, it didn't matter. Even if it wasn't as much as it could have been, it was more. It was profit.

I could see it in Hong's eyes, the same glimmering excitement that I felt. The same delight in progress and self-sufficiency. But there was something else as she sat down on the bench beside me, something else in all of us. Something in the stillness of the sky that lingered above us, always above us, unmoving. In the way the shadow of the bench slowly ushered its way from one side to the other. Something about waiting, waiting. We had been in Sway Siphon for a month now. *How much longer?* we wondered. *When?*

Hong sighed, and in our hearts, we all sighed along with her. But then she turned to me, and there was a look in her eye you didn't often see, not on Hong. "Maybe this time, I'll go," she said.

I sat up. After all, why not? There was nothing else for her to do, and I needed a few days to rest and recover. We could accumulate something for ourselves while we waited. Something weightier to sew into the

Never Again

hems of our shirts. Something we could bring to Thailand with us. Something we could use to start a new life.

"All right," I said, and Hong smiled.

She left early the next morning, shouldering a couple of empty bags and tucking our new wad of baht into her pants. In exchange, she handed me the pearls and ruby that she'd been concealing in her hem. I stitched these into my shirt now, and I watched as she headed off to the edge of town.

The sun rose high in the sky. The shadow of our bench slipped under us until it was hardly a shadow at all. The traders in the market sold their goods, they gathered their money, and they began to pack up. The sun sank low behind the trees, and the shadow of the bench grew long and spindly. We ate our rice that Hong had bought with our profit, and we fell asleep under a starry sky.

Hong didn't arrive in the morning, so I made my siblings some rice, and set aside a serving for Hong when she arrived. But at midday, when the sun was high and the shadow of our bench hid beneath us, there was still no sign of her. We waited. "She probably stopped to rest in the jungle," I told them. "It's a long way to go all in one day."

The sun began to sink. Our shadow slinked to the side of the bench. It grew longer and longer, and at last vanished with the sun. We fell asleep without Hong. "She'll be back tomorrow," I told them, but when they had fallen asleep and I still lay awake, looking up at the vastness of the sky, I worried. *What's taking you so long, Hong?*

The sun rose again in the morning, soft and pink, but Hong was not there. We waited again as the sun

Never Again

climbed higher and higher, and the shadow of the bench shrank beneath it. Again, the market sellers sold their goods, packed up their belongings and left. The shadow beneath us stretched long and thin, and then vanished all together. Night had fallen. Another night without Hong.

Where are you? I wondered, looking at the forest behind which the sun had fled. *What happened?*

Morning rose. I looked to the forest. I watched for my sister.

And that is when they came. It was what we had been waiting for ever since we arrive at Sway Siphon. The man Eang's mom had introduced us to walked up to our bench. He put a hand on my shoulder and whispered in my ear. "It's time. We leave tomorrow before sunrise." His finger pointed at a green hill on the edge of town. "Meet there, just as it gets light. Then we'll leave."

Panic crept over me then with quivering fingers that tightened their quaking grip. "But Hong isn't here!" I said.

The man shrugged. "We leave tomorrow."

I scrambled off to find Eang's mom. "Hong isn't here," I told her. "She left three days ago and hasn't come back!" She looked back at me with concerned eyes, but her answer was the same as the man's. "Get ready to leave, Sida."

So I returned to our bench and told my siblings to get ready. "She'll be back before sunrise," I told them. *Maybe. Maybe she'll be back before sunrise.*

It didn't take long. We wrapped some dried rice, salt, a coconut shell cup, pot, some clothes, a worn black scarf, and our plastic tarp in a bag. My siblings each tied their own clothes into a tight bundle. This was all that we needed. We wanted to travel light. Still there was one thing we had to do before we left.

I told Thy to follow me, and we walked toward the rice fields. I didn't tell her why because I knew she would balk, but it had to be done. Eang's mom had said so. When we reached the swampy edge of the field, I bent down and scooped some of the earth into my palm. It was soft mud and slick. It was perfect. "Smear this across your body," I told her. I spread the first handful across my cheek. It was cold and wet, but it would soon dry.

Thy wrinkled her nose as she watched me. "Why?"

I hesitated, but I could see by the look on her face how repulsed my sister was by the mud. If she was going to do it, she had to know why. "Eang's mom told me we should," I told her. "She said it's dangerous. There are bandits hiding in there, and soldiers." I began to wet my hair with the water from a puddle of mud into my hair, running my fingers through it and then bunching it into wild tangles. "She said they capture the prettiest girls."

I was spreading it over my arms and legs now, a thin coating that dripped down my skin. But Thy was still looking at me with that same look of puzzled disgust. "The uglier we are, the safer," I said. I didn't really understand all this at the time, not like I do now. I had this vague sense of danger, but it wasn't until I was older that I could really understand what Eang's mom had been helping us to avoid.

Thy looked at the mud with much the same look she had once given the leeches she'd witnessed on my legs. But at last, she took a deep breath and reached into the mud. When I was finished, I helped her, scrubbing the mud into her hair and slicking it down her back.

Never Again

When we came back to our bench, we reached into the ashes left by our last fire. These we spread through our hair, gritty enough to do the job, but not impossible to untangle later.

It was the last night we slept on that bench. We spent our last night in Cambodia under a blanket of mud and ash.

I tried to sleep. I knew we needed our rest. But I could not stop thinking it. *Come home tonight, Hong. Come home.* I kept imagining her silhouette stumbling forward in the darkness, fumbling for our bench, her body weighed down by the heavy sacks on her back. I kept watching for her. *Come back, Hong. Come back, now.*

But there was something else bothering me. Something that clung to me like the mud on my skin. Something I had said that day when we had been separated on our road away from the Khmer Rouge, that day when the soldier had driven us away from our siblings and I had been so afraid we wouldn't find them again, and then, miracle of miracles, we had found our way. We had seen them huddled on the side of the road, and I had been so glad to have us all together again. So glad. *Never again.* I had said. *We're not going to separate. Not ever again.*

But here we were.

Come back, Hong. Come back, now!

But she didn't come. And dawn was approaching.

Chapter 26

Danger in the Rice Paddies

I woke my siblings just before sunrise. We were taking only what we needed for the trip. The ruby and pearls were still snuggly stitched into the hem of my shirt. I folded our plastic tarp and stuffed it into my bag. My siblings tied their own bundles onto their backs with their scarves. I slung my own bag over my shoulder, leaving my hands free.

As we prepared, I kept an eye on the road. One last hope that I would see Hong. I did not.

We crept out of the town under the darkness. The mud had dried and cracked now, forming a kind of scaly second skin over my body.

We found Eang and her mom at the top of the hill. There was a group of about sixty people gathered. They were families, clusters that crossed generations. Mothers. Fathers. Grandparents. Children. But there were none as young as Peou.

There was only a vague hint of the sun. A faint glow on the horizon behind us. One you would never see if you didn't know to look for it. Before us, the hill sloped down into a vast green sea of rice plants. The monsoons had been good this season and the rice lush in a pool of rainwater. And beyond them, a faint shadow in the night, the jungle.

A whisper rippled through the crowd. "It's time," it said. "Let's go."

So I took Peou's hand in mine, and we walked down the hill.

Danger in the Rice Patties

When we first stepped into the rice paddies, the water was cool and refreshing, but the mud beneath was slick, and we had to walk carefully lest we slip. Kann and Peou said nothing as we waded deeper into the field. Even Thy did not whimper or complain of her fear of leeches. We were on our way out. We were on our way to freedom. And maybe, just maybe, Hong was somewhere on the other side of those trees. Somewhere safe.

The water was up to my knees now, which meant it came up to Kann's waist, and Peou's chest. She wouldn't be able to go much deeper on her own. The mud was no longer slippery but thick and deep. It molded itself around our feet, reaching between our toes and knotting itself around our ankles so that we had to yank with each step to pull ourselves out. The deeper we walked, the more uneven the ground became, rife with dips and knots and tangles of branches and roots that wrapped cold tendrils around our feet. Because of this we moved slowly.

I pried one foot out of the mud and stepped forward only to find water - water - water. I plunged forward into it, waist-deep. "Wait!" I urged my brother and sister who were still a step behind in shallower water. I felt forward slowly with my feet. The mud rose up higher here, and I found a surface to stand on. I stepped up out of it to where the water only reached to my thighs.

"Careful," I told my siblings. "Step over the ditch." Gingerly they felt forward with their toes and stepped onto the ground next to me. And we continued forward.

Now we moved slowly, testing the mud gently with every step. When we reached a ditch, we paused

Danger in the Rice Patties

and cautiously found our way across it: me first, then Thy and Kann and then Peou. But the water was getting deeper, and before long, Peou was struggling to move through the water, rice greens bobbing about her chin. So I let go of her hand and swung her up over my shoulders. She clung to my head with muddy fingers, and her legs pressed tight against my neck.

The sun had risen now, and morning light spread softly against our backs in in silvery ripples against the surface of the water. It lapped around my hips and Kann's shoulders. Thy slipped along quietly next to us, the water blinking in silken circles around her waist.

That was when we heard it. *Pop!* A sound that split my heart and sent tremors through my bones. *Pop! Pop! Pop!* I didn't have to look back to know what made that noise.

And then the sound that followed. Screams. They erupted around us.

"Come back!" a voice shouted. It was distant, far behind us on dry land. "Come back!"

We were only a third of the way through the field. I looked ahead at the great expanse of water that stretched before us, the rice growing in a thick green net. Could we ever make it through? With soldiers chasing us behind?

But we couldn't go back. Surely, they would shoot us anyway. And there was no life behind us, only a different kind of death. No, this was worth the risk. I had told Hong this weeks before, and I still knew it was true. It was worth the risk.

"Keep going." I told my siblings. "We are going!"

Pop! Pop! Pop! There was a spray of water as the bullets dove into the rice paddies.

Danger in the Rice Patties

We continued our shuffle into the deeper water, but it was quicker now. There was no time for reaching forward to test every step. The moment that took might mean a bullet. Even so, the mud sucked at our feet and the rice plants tied themselves in knots around our legs.

The water itself pushed heavily against us. I was glad, for a moment, for its depth. It provided some cover for us, a watery shield to slow the bullets.

Except for Peou! I realized this suddenly. She was high on my shoulders, above the water, surrounded by nothing but naked air.

I reached up to swing her down to my waist. Her legs gripped me tightly there, and her arms wrapped themselves around my neck. "Go!" I said again, and we moved forward.

The water deepened. It lapped around Kann's chin now. He turned his face up to the sky to keep it from splashing into his mouth. If we stepped into a ditch now, he would be submerged.

The bullets still rang out, blistering the sky and glassy water in front of us, breaking it into hundreds of white shards that burst into the air, bright and flickering, and then rained down on us, sharp and angry.

There were screams and wailing all around us. Cries of fear and bewilderment. Exclamations of terror.

And there were other screams. Ones that were thrust out when a bullet had met its mark. And there were the screams that followed by the surrounding people as they scrambled to reach their loved one, to hold her above the surface of the water.

"Help!" someone cried. "Help me!"

I didn't look to see whether she was pleading for herself or for someone else. If I turned I would only be a better target.

Danger in the Rice Patties

"Don't worry about them," I told Kann and Thy. "Keep moving."

There was a sudden tug at my shoulder. Small fingers scrambling at my arm, pulling me down. It was Kann, his face almost submerged, his lips sputtering. With Peou on one side, I reached for Kann on the other, looping my elbow under his armpit. He gripped my arm with tight fingers, and with the other hand, he held onto my waist. His weight pulled me down until the water reached up to my shoulders. Maybe it was better this way, the water providing more cover, but it made it harder to move.

There was another shriek beside us and then the soft plunk of water closing over a body. I looked over my shoulder to make sure it wasn't Thy. But Thy was still there, moving along silently beside us. Behind her, a woman flailed through water frantically. "My son! My son!" she wailed. "Help me!" And then her words dissolved into a sputter of horror and misery.

I was frozen for a moment. A very brief moment. *Can I just leave her there? How can I leave her?* Because her face was one I'd seen before. I'd seen it even in myself. It was the same face I had worn as I walked home to my mother whom I had known was dead but had hoped was not. And maybe with this boy it was different. Maybe if she had help, he could make it to the jungle. Maybe then he could still make it across the border to freedom. But I knew this hope was in vain.

Then the weight of Peou's body brought me back to myself. And Kann's tight grip on my shoulder. I could not help. I had these two to get to the other side. I had to keep the chain together.

So I turned away from her cries. "Don't look," I told them. "Keep going. We keep going."

Danger in the Rice Patties

The rain of bullets continued, and with them, a second rain of water drops. The latter was a strange, an upside-down rain, water falling up, up, up. But of course, it found gravity eventually, and then it came down on us.

"Hurry!" I told my siblings, though only Thy and I could control our pace, and we were already going as fast as we could.

The water was at my neck now, flecking its spray against Kann's upturned face. *Don't get any deeper.* I found myself pleading with it. Right now, the water was our friend, our shield. But any moment it could turn on us. And if it did, it would be an even fiercer enemy than the soldiers. *Please, please!* I begged. *No deeper.*

In our haste we stepped into it. A depression in the field, a low spot. We experienced it only as water. Water around and above us. Water in our hair and nose and lungs. And there were other things too. The ribbons of rice leaves. The tangle of arms and legs. Kann's fingers looped around mine. Peou's grip still tight around my neck.

But I had been here before. Back at the river in Steang Chas. In the swirl of water and the flashes of sunlight, bent and moving. I had made it out that time. And now I knew the way. Now I knew that there was ground below and I only had to find it.

So I did. My feet reached until they found mud. They gripped the mud and pushed. One step. Then another. We burst out again. Into air. Into sunlight. Into the spray of bullet-ridden water. "Keep moving!" I said, when my lungs were full of air again and I was able to speak. I could see it up ahead. A bank. It was mud at first but then grass and a tangle of trees. The jungle.

Danger in the Rice Patties

There was an end to this. If we kept moving, we would reach it. If we kept moving.

There were splashes and wet sucking sounds as bodies around us sank beneath its surface. The wild patter of bullets still splattering the water.

We were more than halfway across now. "Keep going," I told them. I would say it again and again. I would say it until we were across. Until we reached Thailand. Until we were free.

Kann's hands clasped tightly around my shoulder, and Peou's knees were so firmly pressed into my stomach that at any other time I would have winced, but now I was glad for the fierceness of their grips. It meant that I only had to move, that if I just kept going, kept going, we would make it.

The water was slowly slipping away from us, now. I could see Kann's neck, and the hand with which he clung to me was loosening its grip.

Bullets were still hurling themselves into the water, but they were fewer than before, and most of them struck behind us.

I could make out the individual trees ahead now. The morning light drew them into clear lines, separate trunks and branches. Those trees would catch and swallow a bullet. If we could make it behind them, we would be safe.

At last, Kann was able to let go and walk on his own, but he followed close behind me, careful to match my footfall with his. Thy was still at our side, moving with an almost rhythmic grace between the rice plants.

When I stepped into another low spot, the water rising suddenly to my chest, I turned. "Wait!" I reached until my toes found higher ground. "Here," I told Kann. "Follow me." And I stepped forward. He stepped exactly where I had, reaching one hand forward to cling to me.

"Keep going," I told them again. The water only reached to Kann's chest now. And then his waist.

Now that the water was shallower, we moved faster, but I was aware of the shield we were losing. There was more body for the bullets to strike. The mud still clung to our feet with tenacious grip, but we yanked ourselves away from it again and again.

I set Peou down on her feet now. The water only reached to her waist.

"Run!" I told them. "Run!"

It was hard to do, the mud still sucking at our feet. But the edge was close now. And then solid ground. And behind that, trees. And behind those, freedom.

The bullets were only a thin spray now. But it only took one to break a body open. And there would be no crossing the border with a muddy bullet wound.

We ran. The ground sloped up toward the jungle. There the trees stood like family. Their arms spread wide. Ready to wrap themselves around you. Guard you. If only you could get to them first.

Freed from the weight of the water and the heavy cling of mud, we were fast. It felt as though we were flying, like the bullets that flung themselves through the air behind and beside us. We ran until we reached the first tree. It wasn't enough. "Keep going! Keep running!" I cried. "Follow me."

So we ran until more trees closed in behind us. We ran until they formed a thick wall. Till they blocked out the sky and the bright sunlight and the sight of the rice paddies.

And then we stopped. We collapsed onto the ground. Air thundered in and out of our lungs, and our entire bodies quaked with both relief and terror. *We made it! We made it.*

    We stayed there a long time until our breath had slowed and our hearts calmed. Then we sat up and looked around. Through the trees we could see movement. Others from our group. We rose and followed them slowly, tenderly with aching feet and legs that still trembled. From around the edge of the forest, we gathered. There were only about forty of us now. And I was so relieved to have made it, so grateful to have my three siblings still by my side, that I didn't notice that Eang's mom and her children were not among them.

Chapter 27

Like Mist into Rain

We found a road in the forest. It was a narrow dirt road between trees, cut by buffalo-drawn carts. Their wheels had left deep trenches in the mud, trenches that led all the way to Thailand. This would be our path now. The word was passed quietly through the group. "Stay on the path," alongside other phrases like "land mines" and "all over the jungle." I remembered Ny, that first death so long ago. Like a doorway from one world to another, this nightmare we'd been living since. I remembered the way her foot had vanished somehow, swallowed up by the landmine. I remembered how close I had been.

What would happen if I lost my leg like she did? I thought it out, imagining the scenario. Thy and Kann leaning over me with anxious faces. *Would they leave me behind? Would they be able to make it the rest of the way on their own? Would they stay and die with me? Because surely I would die as Ny had. There was no way to survive in this world without a leg.*

So we walked along the path. I trudged through one trench. Peou walked behind me, then Kann, then Thy. Each stepped in my footprints. In the other trench, on the other side of a grassy mound that swelled high and green between the two ruts, our fellow travelers walked. They were strangers, and yet they were the closest thing to friends that we had now. The closest thing to family.

Like Mist into Rain

The air was heavy with moisture. It was thick and clumsy as it lumbered into our lungs, and it clung with invisible weight to our skin.

At midday, we stopped and ate some dried rice that was now swollen from the water in the rice paddies. We sprinkled this with salt. My siblings ate quietly. They didn't complain that they were tired or that their feet ached. They, too, believed that all this would be worth it. After we had eaten, I searched along the path for water. The ground was soft and the water buffalo who had last tread it had left deep cloven prints like delicate cups in the ground, the shape of a two-petaled lotus. It had rained since he had passed, and water had filled these cups. Time and stillness had cleaned the water, letting the dirt drift down and leaving the surface clear and glistening. I used our coconut shell to skim the top of the water. I had to be careful not to touch the edges or to trouble the water or the dirt would stir itself back in. We had to drain them as gently as if they were fine china.

When everyone had drunk enough, Thy and I reached into the puddles for some extra mud to smear on our bodies. Much of the ash and mud had been washed away in the rice paddies. A thin film of silt still coated our bodies, but to be safe we wanted to cover ourselves with more.

Above us, the forest's leafy roof covered the sky, but every now and then, when the wind moved just right, the sunlight would slip through in trembling golden splotches. It would dance upon the ground for a moment, and then it was gone.

The group began to move again, and we followed. Sometimes there were obstacles. A fallen tree, a large root, a swollen puddle. We always climbed over these; we never went around. We never strayed from the path.

When it happened, it happened suddenly. We had been walking under the quiet of the trees. And then suddenly there were the black cotton uniforms. The dark scarves and the military caps. The guns. *Oh no! Not again!* I didn't know where they had come from. They must have been hiding in the trees, but now they surrounded us. There were probably ten of them, each loaded down with guns. Some held riffles, others had shoulder rockets or grenade launches perched over their shoulders. The weight of these guns looked oppressive. And yet if you held a gun, you ruled the world.

Everyone in front of us had already dropped to the ground, and now we did the same, each of us sitting on the dirt, hugging our knees and bowing our heads to their weapons.

It had been months since we'd seen the Khmer Rouge. We hadn't forgotten to fear them, but it was a fear that I was weary of. After years of being of afraid of them, after months of feeling I had escaped. *After all this time, all this running, we're back here again. Back to the beginning. And after all this time, what will happen? Will they capture me, take me away? And what of Thy and Kann and Peou? After all this hard work, will we die here?*

They must have been speaking. Must have made some demands of the others. I did not hear their voices. They must have been stepping around us, their rubber tire sandals smacking the mud. I did not hear them. I could only hear my own heartbeat.

My heart was pounding loud enough, you would have thought the earth was quaking, but it was me. Or perhaps it was the earth after all. Splitting apart with each *thud! thud! thud!* This earth that had brought the Khmer Rouge to us in the first place. That had led their boots all the way to Phnom Penh. That had submitted to the Khmer Rouge when they ordered it to grow rice. That had allowed children to plow it, children to plant it, children to harvest it. And then it had opened itself up willingly for their wasted bodies. We had laid my brother down inside the earth, and it had not protested or wept. It had willingly spread itself over his body in burial. And then my mother. It had opened itself to her, too. And then my father, had it soaked up his blood silently?

But now here in the jungle, on the very brink of freedom, these Khmer Rouge stood over us again, and it was they who would determine if we lived or died. After years of silence, maybe, the earth was breaking. Maybe it was the ground that was trembling and not me. But even if this were so, the earth could not save us. We were at their mercy. And when had the Khmer Rouge ever shown mercy. *We are dead*, I thought. *They will rob us. They will kill us. We won't make it out this time. We are dead.*

It was the waiting I couldn't stand. It stirred the fear that shook me into an uncontainable froth until I was afraid I would burst.

There was a twig in front of me. Just inches from my feet. I reached for it with trembling fingers. I only needed something to hold. Something to look at it. I grasped it in my hand and began to scratch. Bit by bit, I carved a little hole in the ground. With each scrape across the soil, with each little grain dislodged, something came back to me. Something I couldn't put into words. Something that I had known but that the fear had made me forget. Something about not being alone. Something about someone watching.

Like Mist into Rain

I wasn't quite sure what it was, this thing that was returning to me. But as it came, I began to pray. *Oh God, please help us. Please help us!* With every scratch in the dirt, I prayed it. And it became a new kind of rhythm. One more steady than my racing heart. *God, help us. God, help us. God, help us.*

One of the men came towards me then. I could only see his feet. Those black tire sandals. The kind they had probably worn when they killed my father. They stopped right in front of me. They waited.

I said nothing. I only kept digging with the stick. *God, help us. God, help us. God, help us.*

Slowly, it all faded from my mind. The feet. The tire sandals. The guns. I could see nothing before me but the soft dirt and my little twig. I kept digging. I kept praying.

I don't know how long I was there, digging and praying, but a voice suddenly shook me from my trance. "It's okay!" it said. "We can go now." They were incomprehensible words. How could it be okay? How could we be allowed to go? I looked up and saw that everyone else was already on their feet. Their packs were already loaded back onto their backs. There was not a black uniform or a gun in sight. *But why?* I didn't understand. It didn't make sense. Why would the Khmer Rouge let us go like that? *Why am I still alive?*

There was no time to answer the question. The group was already moving. I rose and quickly grabbed my bag. I followed the others down the road, and my siblings followed me, but my mind was still whirling.

It wasn't long before we came across a smell that I knew well. A smell that meant others before us had not been as fortunate as we were. Their bodies had been dragged to the side of the trail, but not far enough that we couldn't see them. It was a cluster of three. I looked away. I had seen enough of death.

This thing was still troubling me. It didn't make sense. Why wasn't I lying under the brush with them? It was then that I really began to remember. I fumbled to put it into words. I had begun to put it together back at the temple, when I had knelt before the broken statue, but what had been vague and ghostly was becoming more concrete. Like mist condensing into rain. I could almost see it. Could almost feel it falling, droplets on my skin. It was real. There was someone watching us. Someone taking care of us. We were not alone.

It was an overwhelming thought, both beautiful and terrifying. And so hard to justify. Why should I live and not they? Why Sida and not Chao? And there was a danger to it too, a darkness. Such thoughts could never be spoken. "You think God is watching over you?" they might spit. "Let's see how that turns out!" and they would laugh, but it would be a bitter and angry laugh because they too would have lost so many whom they'd loved. I couldn't answer the question why. And I couldn't explain how it worked. I only knew it was true. And I had to keep it a secret.

That night, it rained. We had stopped when the forest had become so dark you couldn't see your next step. The leaves above us were so thick, not even the slenderest thread of moonlight could slip through them. We only had one tarp, so we laid ourselves out on the mud and spread the plastic across our bodies like a blanket. We had to press in against one another to fit, and even so, the tarp would not stretch across my feet. I had to hold one corner down with my fist, and another with my toes. On the other side, Thy was doing the same.

Like Mist into Rain

    Still, the rain splashed down in big wet drops. I couldn't see them for the darkness, but I could feel them dribbling down my skin. I could smell them. I could taste them in the heaviness of the air. I could hear them tapping out a drumbeat on the tarp. I knew they were there.

Chapter 28

Five Links in a Chain

When we woke in the morning, we were soaked. The tarp had shifted during the night, and it lay in a useless rumple to one side. We were shivering as we sat up, and yet we couldn't stop smiling. The rain had stopped, and the morning light was peaking through the trees. Even the jungle knew what we knew, that today we would reach Thailand. We shook out the tarp and folded it. We ate a hasty breakfast, and then we rose and continued down the path.

"Not much longer," someone said. And we all smiled.

"Not much longer," they said half an hour later.

"Very close now," they said a while after that.

It was always close. Because if it was always close, we could always manage a few more steps. If it was always close, we would always have the joy and excitement of being so near.

We hurried along down the path with the eagerness of someone who was almost at her destination. In my haste, I stumbled across a root. There was only time for a mere glance at my heal and the gash that cut an inch into it. But we were so close. So I kept going.

It was about noon when we came to the giant log. It had to have been about two feet wide and fifteen feet long. It crossed the whole path, and –unwilling to stray from the path for fear of the land mines—we had to climb over it. Thy and Kann made it over themselves, but I had to help Peou across. Just a few steps past the log, we could see it. It was a metal sign with letters. We couldn't read them, but we knew that they weren't the thick swooping characters that we had grown up reading. It wasn't Khmer. They were the delicate curls of the Thai language.

"We're in Thailand!" someone cried out.

"Where is the border?" someone else asked.

There was a line scraped into the dirt across the path. A couple inches thick, an indentation in the soil. "There it is!" someone cried.

We looked at it in wonder. This was what freedom looked like. The scratching of a stick into soil. We each took our turns crossing it. It was not a mere step. I raised one leg high and with deliberation reached across the line, then I lowered it, and my foot landed on Thai soil. Free soil. Then my next foot left Cambodia, rose high over the border, and then came down onto Thailand. Behind me came Peou, Kann, and Thy. They each did the same, one big step.

There was cause for celebration. We laughed. We hugged one another. Not just our families but everyone in the group. We had done this together. We were laughing, cheering, and clapping. "Finally! We have crossed the line!" someone cried. It was as though crossing this line, we had crossed out of fear. As though there was no more need for silence. The line was magic. It meant freedom. In the midst of the cheers, I heard a woman's voice shout out "Preah ban chuoy yeau hide!" It was Khmer for "God has helped us!" I wondered at these words. The truth in them surged inside me, something as powerful as the joy of our accomplishment. And there was something else. The reality that I was not alone. That I was not the only one with this secret

Five Links in a Chain

thought forming in my mind. That I was not the only one He was watching.

This is the moment I like to come back to. It was the happiest one. In all four years since the bombs had come to Phnom Penh, in all the fear, the pain, the sorrow, this is the moment where joy reached its peak. We knew now that we were free. But that wasn't all. This was not only the end of everything we'd left, but it was something new. It was a new beginning. A start of life.

We weren't in a rush anymore. We had reached freedom. So we stopped to eat. It was a simple meal of dried rice crumbs, but in the spirit of celebration, it was a feast.

We resumed our walk with renewed energy. The path continued through the forest. Through the flickering green of trees. Through the warm sticky air that clung to our bodies like our wet clothes. It turned out that Thailand looked exactly the same as Cambodia. We walked another hour. Our feet ached. Our legs were heavy. Our heads were swimming with hope and hunger. We walked another hour. Still there was nothing but jungle. Where was Thailand? Where were its lush fields? Its towns? Its people? Its refugee camps that we'd heard of, opening their arms to people like us. We were beginning to worry.

But then trees thinned. Bit by bit they fell away. And then we could see it. A bamboo hut with its thatched roof. Like the one I had built with my father back in Cambodia, except bigger. And then there was another. And another. It was a town! Around the huts, the trees were sparse. Plenty of room for light and wide patches of sky. We had made it.

Behind the cluster of huts, we saw a foreign sight. Two large buses. I hadn't seen vehicles that big since before the war. "Those are for us," someone said, pointing. "To take us to the refugee camps," they said. It was like a dream. Could it be so easy? Buses to safety?

There was a pond on the way into the town, and I stopped to wash my foot in its water. The cut had filled with mud, and I dug it out with a stick till it was clear. Then I rose to my feet. "Come on," I said. "Let's go look for Hong."

It was only hope. After all, anything could have happened to Hong. She could have been captured by the Vietnamese as I had, only they may not have decided to let her go. Or she might have fallen and been injured as that one man had, and they may have left her behind. She may have gotten lost in the jungle, or she may have been found by the Khmer Rouge as we were, only they may not have decided to spare her. She could be anywhere. But anywhere included here. And I had to hope. And hope had led me to good things so far.

The rest of the group had already dispersed, headed to the buses or found contacts or gone wherever they had intended to go. We had to hurry. The sun was slinking towards the horizon, and the buses would surely be leaving soon. This might be our only chance. But we had to find Hong. And if we didn't, would we ever see her again?

We stopped at a mango tree on the edge of town. From beneath its wide branches, it divided the village into two sides. "Thy and Kann, you go that way," I pointed to the southern half of the town. "Look for Hong, and then in five minutes come back here." They nodded. "Peou and I will look on this side." I pointed to the northern half. "No matter what happens, in five minutes be back here at this tree." Again, they nodded.

Five Links in a Chain

"Do you understand? Right here in five minutes. No matter what!"

So we went our separate ways. With Peou's hand in mine, we walked through the town. We peered into each hut, scanned each face. *Not Hong, not Hong, not Hong*, I found myself thinking as I checked each woman I saw. Here we were again, looking for Hong. Here we were, trying to link our golden chain back together, what links were left. The more we looked, the more I began to worry. She wasn't here. We weren't going to find her. And when the five minutes were up, what then? Would we board the bus without her? Would we give up? Never see her again? Never find out what had happened?

Yes, we had to. We had to get on those buses. It might be our only chance.

And yet I didn't know if I could.

Five minutes had passed. Peou and I walked back to the tree. It stood alone under the fading sky. We waited to see Thy and Kann's slender forms coming up from the village. But we did not see them. We waited and waited. And while we waited the sky blushed orange like a mango.

My heart began to stutter a wilder and wilder beat, and my hands were trembling again. I had to go looking for them. And yet if we left this tree and they came back here as they had promised…

Why wouldn't they return after five minutes? After I had said so so firmly? Why wouldn't they return?

Something must have happened. It was the only conclusion to draw. And now the buses were there, but they would leave any minute. I had to find them and get on the buses. *But what about Hong?* There was a wildness taking over me. Panic and trembling. "Never again," we had said. We had said we would not separate, not ever again. So *how are we here again? How could I have lost them?*

I took Peou's hand and began to run. We dashed to the southern side of the town, Peou scrambling a step behind me. I peered around the first hut, and then behind the second. But the tree was nagging at me now. *What if they've returned to the tree?*

So I ran back towards the tree, dragging Peou behind. But its shade was still empty. They were not there.

Two or three times, I ran back and forth. Looking in the village, looking at the tree. *Thy! Kann! What has happened to you?*

It was on the third trip back to the tree that I saw them. Thy and Kann were running towards me, and there were smiles on their faces. I was overcome with both a fierce urge to scold them and an aching relief, desperate to fling my arms around them, and these things blinded me at first to the meaning of their smiles. "We found her! We found her!" They cried once they were near. "We found Hong!"

"Where?" I clasped my arm around each of them in a quick embrace. There was no time to linger.

"Follow us!"

So we followed them back into the village and to the doorway of a hut. Of course, she was cooking when I came upon her. I saw her back only, a straight line as she knelt before a boiling pot, her knees forming a crisp angle. She was blowing on the fire. Her hair, too, was a straight line of black falling down her back, the orange glow of the fire folding itself into golden creases down her hair. I would know that deliberate kind of beauty, that meticulous precision anywhere. It was my sister.

Five Links in a Chain

"Hong!" I cried, and she turned. Her lips spreading in a smile, she came to me, and I flung my arms around her neck. Tears dribbled down my muddy checks, and all the dirt and ashes on my filthy clothes pressed against hers. I almost expected to hear her chide, "Sida! You're so dirty!" But she didn't. She only held as tightly onto me as I had held onto her.

When she did speak, it was in a rush. "I came here and spent all the money as planned, but I got tired on the way back, so we stopped to rest, and when I woke up, everything was gone. I had been robbed, and I didn't know the way by myself, and I had nothing to eat, so I came back, and this family let me work for them, and I just hoped you would come and that you'd find me when you did, and you did—you found me!"

"We have to go!" I said, releasing her at last. "Before it's too late."

"Okay," Hong said, wiping tears from her cheeks, while Peou and the others reached in for their own hurried embraces. "I'll go tell them I'm leaving."

Hong walked across to a woman on the other side of the hut, spoke quietly to her, and then returned. "Let's go."

So the five of us we walked toward the refugee buses, hand in hand. Five links in a chain. It was all that remained of the Kong family. But we were together.

Chapter 29

The Reason I Was Alive

When we approached the buses, I began to worry again. It seemed too good to be true. I found myself wondering: *What if they don't take you to the refugee camp? What if they tell you that's where you are going, but they're lying and you just walk onto their bus?* I had heard of this happening. Of buses that lured refugees in only to drive them back over the border where they'd come from. Or worse, driving them to the mountain only to send them over the edge. *How can I know if it's safe?* There was a man stepping off the bus in front. I recognized the letters on his shirt as European letters, letters not from our alphabet. Only later did I learn that the letters "U. N." meant United Nations. He gestured to us pointing to the bus, welcoming us on. *It might be a trap.* And yet, it was the only way. It was worth the risk.

So we got on the bus.

The bus drove us to our first refugee camp, Khao I Dang (KID). I remember the crowd that had gathered at the gate with hopeful faces. They peered into the bus, looking for someone they knew and loved. I would join that crowd a few days later, looking hopefully at every new load of passengers, hoping to see the face of Chun or my father, but each time I would be disappointed.

Once we got off the bus, we were divided into groups. Each group was assigned a leader. Ours approached Hong and me with a piece of paper and a pen. "You are together?" He gestured towards my siblings, and I nodded. "How many?" he asked.

The Reason I Was Alive

"Five," I told him.

He took our names. "And how old are you?" he asked.

"Fourteen," I told him.

When he pointed to the others, I rattled off their ages, too.

Once everyone had been registered on that list, we were driven to a field in Section V and told that this would be our new home.

Night fell. We slept our first night of freedom under the stars. An open sky with no borders. The next morning, we began to build our home, a bamboo hut. It was just like the one we had built in Steang Chas those years before. Only this time my father and Chun were not there to reach the center of the roof and to lift the heaviest beams. The group leader helped us with the hardest things, and Kann stood on my shoulders when we needed to reach the highest places. Then we made ourselves a bed of bamboo. It was the first bed we had slept on since before our parents were gone, and we took great delight in it, lounging across it in luxury, rubbing our backs across the smooth curves of bamboo. Every three days we were brought a new ration of food which we cooked and ate. It was a comfortable life and safe. But we wondered how long we would be here. We wondered what was next.

It wasn't long before the camp orphanage heard about us and came to get us. My siblings and I climbed into their motor cart and rode away. I remember the crowds that watched us in awe. Going somewhere new, to a better life.

At the orphanage, we found a whole world of things we had forgotten. We were given a welcome kit that included soap, a tooth brush, a notebook, and pen.

The Reason I Was Alive

These were things we hadn't seen since Phnom Penh, memories of an ancient time. Food was prepared for us and served in a dining room. It was more than just rice and fish – which was pretty much all we'd eaten since we left the temple. What's more, there were no rations. We ate as much as we pleased and, when they noticed the ravenous appetite with which we devoured our servings, they leaned forward and offered us more. We were sent to school where we resumed our education after four years. We were assigned to a house mom, who looked after a group of ten children, and we all slept on one big bamboo bed. Most luxurious of all, we had access to a shower with running water and an enclosure for privacy. Each of us took our turn in this shower, cleanliness accessible at the turn of a knob.

There was a happiness and security at this place that we hadn't known for so long. And there was a new kind of freedom, one I hadn't felt since that day two years before when the boy had whispered in my ear, when he had told me about my father. I didn't have to be a mother anymore. I didn't have to be responsible for my siblings. They were taken care of. *I* was taken care of. I could be a child again.

One night, I was lying in bed. All the others had fallen asleep, but I was awake. It was dark, the sun having long since set, and if there was a moon that night, it was hiding. I remember how silent it was. Not the twitter of a bird. Not the hush of the wind. It was as if even the air was asleep.

It was in that silence, in that darkness, that I heard the song. It was soft at first, barely discernible, but gradually it grew louder. Voices were singing, I could tell that, but I couldn't make out the words. Only the

The Reason I Was Alive

quiet rise and fall of the tune. It was a gentle melody with a soft but constant rhythm.

There is no more peaceful sound than the sound of that song. It rolled into the room like a brook rolls through a forest, with the quiet pouring of its presence. And with the song, came something else, too. I could feel it, washing over me. It was not something, but Someone. A presence. Someone watching me.

But while all this felt new, I could tell, somehow that it wasn't. It was familiar, a presence I had felt before, only I hadn't known it. I closed my eyes and remembered. I remembered lying on the floor of the hut, my body shaking with fever. "God, help me," I had prayed. And I remembered the rush of corn stalks, the pound of dirt against my knees as I knelt before the spy boys and waited for the end. I remembered lying in the darkness, with Peou at my side, I remembered the terror I had felt, certain she would be found and they would take us all away. I remembered standing at the fork in the road. Two winding paths that disappeared into endless brush and the thudding of my heart. *Which way do I go?* I remembered that little stick, and how I had dug and dug at the ground. I remembered those feet in the tire sandals and how they had passed me by, and somehow, in these memories, I recognized the presence. This Someone who was here with me now, this Someone whose presence sang out from the notes in that song, He was there. He was there the whole time. He was the reason I was alive.

The enormity of this realization overwhelmed me, but despite its vastness, it was not burdensome. Instead, it lifted a weight from me. The air became lighter. The world became lighter. Suddenly I was so free, so unshackled, if I'd wanted to, I'm sure I could have drifted away. Because for the first time, I didn't need to figure out the next step. For the first time, I didn't have to worry if we were safe. I didn't need to work my way to anything. I didn't need to escape anything. I didn't need to fight to survive. He was doing all that for me. And He was here.

The song played three times, and after the third time, the night drifted back into silence. But the presence stayed. It stretched over me like a bird's wing protects a chick. Like moonlight pierces a dark and hopeless night. Like sunlight gently splashing through river water. I fell asleep.

The next morning, I asked around. "Did you hear anything last night? Did you hear that song?"

The only one who had an answer for me was my house mother, who was helping us get ready for school. "Oh, there's a church over there," she said pointing. "Across from the school."

After school I walked to the neighboring building.

The church was mostly open air, with one wall at the front. There were several rows of benches arranged neatly in the shade of the roof. There was a cross at the front, two pieces of bamboo poised as perpendicular lines. It wasn't a symbol that I recognized, and I wondered what it meant. A few ladies sat in the benches at the front. They held books in their laps, but they leaned toward one another in casual conversation, gesturing from time to time at the pages before them. They didn't take notice of me at first, and it seemed rude to interrupt them, so I wandered through the benches aimlessly for a while. I hoped that they would pause and address me, but they didn't. So I became more bold. I edged toward them slowly until I was only a row behind. Then one of them looked up from the book in her lap and fixed her eyes on me. She smiled a wide, white smile. "Hello!"

"What is this place?" I asked because I'd never seen anything like it before.

"This is a church. God's house. A Christian place," she explained.

Christian. I had heard the word before. It was a fuzzy memory. Something from long before the war.

"You should come in the evenings," she continued. "We read the Bible, sing songs, worship God. You would be welcome." She was still smiling. They all were.

"I heard some singing last night. Was that you?"

"Yes," she nodded. "We often sing. We sing praises to God." She reached forward and lifted a book from one of the benches. She opened the book and pointed to one of the pages. "See. These are the songs that we sing."

I looked at the open page. There were Khmer letters, but my reading was still rusty. I was still struggling in school to piece the sounds together. But above the words was an entirely different kind of writing. Circles and lines. They rolled up and down on the page like a melody. She held the book closer to me. "Take it," she said. "It's yours."

I hesitated at first. It seemed too great a gift. But then my eagerness got the better of me, and I took the book in my own hands. It was the first book I had held in years.

I carried that hymnal home with me that night. It would be months before I could read any of the words in it, but there was something wonderful about the crinkle of the old, worn pages. Something lovely in the way they flicked across my fingers when I flipped through them. Something beautiful about the songs that it contained even if I couldn't yet reach them.

I came back to the church as often as I could. After school, I would sneak in. Hong would cover for me in the orphanage, making up an explanation for my lateness. And I would be in God's house. There were more people there when I returned. Sometimes they read from the Bible, which was their holy book. Sometimes they told me stories about this God and about the man named Jesus who once took five loaves of bread and three fish and turned it into enough food for thousands of people. I listened with awe to that story, my eyes and my mouth wide. That was not something people could do. If we could, imagine the loaves and the fish we would have multiplied back in the work camps. No, only God could do something like that. And a God who could do that, that was the kind of God I wanted to serve.

But when the stories were done, and the Bibles put away, they would sing, their hymnals open, and I would join in and sing along. Slowly I learned the words to the song they sang most often, the song that I had heard that night from my bed, penned by John Newton.

Amazing Grace, How sweet the sound!
That saved a wretch like me.
I once was lost but now am found,
Was blind, but now I see.

T'was Grace that taught my heart to fear,
And Grace, my fears relieved;
How precious did that grace appear
The hour I first believed.

The Reason I Was Alive

The Lord hath promised good to me.
His word my hope secures.
He will my shield and portion be
As long as life endures.

Through many dangers, toils and snares
We have already come.
T'was grace that brought us safe thus far
And grace will lead us home.

Epilogue

In Cambodia, we have a saying: you can cut the grass above the ground, but rain will fall, winds will blow, and it will come back alive. And that is what we did. We came back alive.

After about two years in Thai refugee camps, we found ourselves on another continent, North America. Five Kong children still together. Five links in a chain. Alive.

We were standing in a church. It was a very different kind of church from the one in the refugee camp. This one had walls and beautiful windows that were pieced in color so that the sunshine came in in ribbons of red and blue and yellow. Up in the front there was a cross, but it wasn't made of bamboo, and it wasn't two simple lines. This cross had the figure of Jesus on it. Just as in the church before, we were singing. But when we sang, there was an organ that played deep and reverberating tones that sent vibrations through my bones with every note. Like the church in Thailand, this one taught us stories of Jesus. The service was led by a priest who read passages from the Bible and served wine and wafers, which we weren't allowed to eat because we weren't confirmed Catholics. Instead, they fed mc the one thing I really hungered for: the answer to the question *Who was this God who had looked after me all those years in Cambodia?*

In this church, we were standing, all five of us in a row as we sang together. And beside us sat the Spiveys, an American family. We had been sitting with them late the night before at their dinner table, laughing

Epilogue

and teasing one another. They did that often, brought us into their home, made us feel like family. Loved and looked after.

When the service had ended, they walked with us out the church door and across the grass to the Sunday School building where donuts were always served. When the church had sponsored us, brought us from the refugee camp and offered to take care of us, they had rented out a house for us to live in. The Spiveys weren't the only ones who had volunteered to take care of us. Eight other families had stepped up to meet our various needs. There was Miriam, our English tutor who had also taught us how to light our gas stove, and Elaine who sorted out all the paperwork to get us each enrolled in school. There was Tom who tutored us in math and Sandy who took us all to our dentist and doctor's appointments and Eugene who helped us with all the paperwork. We were in a new country with a new language and a new culture, and everything had seemed strange when we first arrived, but these people were here to help us figure it out. All nine families liked to check in on us each Sunday.

I greeted them cheerfully as I picked up a donut. "Sida!" Elaine called me toward her with a smile and a graceful wave of her hand. Like my mother, everything Elaine did was graceful. She was my English teacher at the high school, and she also tutored me once or twice a week, showing me how to arrange my commas and apostrophes in their correct positions. In the hands of Elaine, even punctuation became like a song, beautiful and precise. "How are you?" she asked, laying her slender fingers on my wrist.

When I first sat in Elaine's classroom, I had been terrified. The other students had read aloud from a play.

Epilogue

The words had rolled off their tongues like music, and they had added to them enthusiasm and expression. Those words, I could tell, must have meant something powerful to those who could understand them, but I could not, and they washed over me, empty and confusing. When class was over, I had waited for all the other students to leave, and then I had stepped up to her desk. Before I could even form the question, she knew what I wanted to say. "Don't worry, Sida," she said with that kind smile, a horizontal parenthesis, "Just listen. It will come." And just like that, my worry had trailed away.

Now, as I ate my donut and talked with Elaine, she listened, nodding. And when she nodded, her hair, an abundance of curls arranged perfectly like commas around her face, nodded in unison.

Across the room Thy was talking to Sandy. Even as she listened, her head angled to one side, I could see a delicate smile on her face. Thy was slowly finding herself at ease again in this world without leeches and parasites. She took comfort in the ready availability of soap, toothpaste, and other guarantors of hygiene. Beside her, Peou stood quietly. Always quietly. Peou would remain that way for many years, hesitant to speak or draw attention to herself.

In the corner, Hong was telling Eugene about her week at school. As she spoke, her hands moved with the same crisp movements that had always characterized my big sister. She approached everything with the same holy precision with which she lit incense before the ancestors, something she would continue to do to that day. While I had come to worship the God of whose "Amazing Grace" I had heard sung in these churches, my sister would continue to worship as our mother and

Epilogue

father had once taught us back in the temple in Phnom Penh.

Kann, next to me, was talking with Tom. Tom, who always liked to tease, was pointing behind my brother. "There's something on your back," he was saying, and Kann was craning his neck to see. "Just kidding!" Tom said, and they both bubbled up in laughter.

I watched my brother laugh. It was a beautiful thing, the way his mouth opened wide, like – for that one instant – all sorrow had fallen away from the world. All around the room my siblings were doing it – if not laughing, smiling. The weight of our past slowly slipped way. And all the while I ate the donut, savoring its sweet chocolate glaze. When I was finished, it wasn't really gone. The glaze had left a thin coat of sticky sweet on my fingers.

It would be years before we found answers to the questions about our family back in Cambodia. Years before I knew for certain that Chun and my father had died. Years before I heard from Eang and her mom that they had survived the rice paddies after all and had followed a different jungle path across the border, that they, too, had eventually made it to America. It would be years before I learned of cousins and an uncle who had survived. Years before I went back to Cambodia to see them.

But for now, these were not the questions on my mind. I licked my fingers, marveling at every sugary glimmer on my fingertips. The families around me gave me hugs, patted my back, put a hand on my shoulder. For now, I was here. I had a new home. I was surrounded by people who loved me.

Epilogue

We had lost one family but gained nine. Dozens of links in a chain.

Photos

Khao I Dang (KID) Refugee Camp

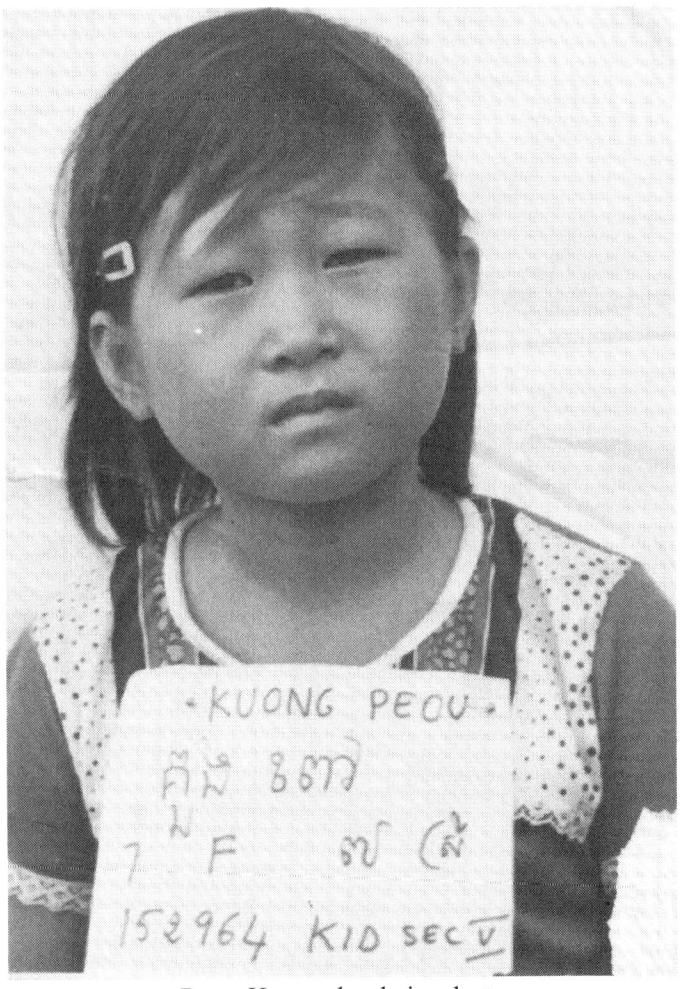

Peou Kong check-in photo
Kong family was assigned to live
in Section V.

Photos

Khao I Dang (KID) Refugee Camp

Camp houses at the base of the mountain

Children at play

Photos

Khao I Dang (KID) Refugee Camp

Hut house

Gathering in the shade by the hospital fence

Photos

Ban Mai Rut Refugee Camp

Thy, Peou, Sida, Kann, and Hong

Sras Kao Refugee Camp

Peou, Sida, Hong, Thy, and Kann

Photos

Cambodia 2009

Thatched hut for about 12 people
Hammocks were only for Mei Kong.

Hut with walls for work camps managers
or Mei Kong

Photos

Cambodia 2009

Rice plants
Heading out

Stubble field
after harvest

Acknowledgements

To all the people who have touched my life:

Saint Margaret Mary church-parish, Rochester, NY

My family: Jonathan, Serena, Sean, Sarah

Oeurn L H., Marie U., Song U., Jessica U., Eileen K., George W., Patricia W., Raymond W., Steve., K., Pauline L., Jack L., Emai L., James L., Edward L., Thomas L., Elaine R., William T., Mariam G., John G., Katherine G., Mariam S., Garry S., Robert S., Carol E., Warner E., Christin E., Paul E., Sandy C., Eugene S., Paul C., CJ S.,

Dong, Chhay Sroeung., Sary O., Narine C., Thai C., Courtney C., Dara C., Randy C., Jennifer C., Sang C., Myles C., Riley C., Rodney C, Brittani C., Paxton C., Poury L., Sonika L., Olivia L., Anna L., Sothy L., Mazlina L., Zackery L., Elias L., Trapiavy D., Dararak R., Villy C., Quoc-Viet C., Saree C., Jack C., Snou B., Shellee B., Baby B., Srean L., Tim L., Pov L., Pauline L.,

Kim L., Lyanna S., Santo K., Victory S., Vincent S., Venerath S., Chris S., Nick K., Moly K., Sophie K., Kari K., Sovia K Neoun Heng K., Ponnamy K., Sot K., Chanda K., Justin K., Elise K., Caylee S., Brooklyn K., Emme K., Navan S., Harry S., Sarath S., Monika Z., Christopher Z., Darin S., Keosha S., Kissouri S., Nakiri S., Leang Cheang, Samedy C., Pov C., Darin C.,

Michael C., Kheang H., Kheng C., Lon C., Eang E., Leap E.,

Tracy F., Joseph F., Joe F., Megan F., Cynthia P., Fernando P., Juanfer P., Juanda P., Andre P., Ariana P., Apichada A., Tanee A., Jason A., Taylor A., Rieke F., Billy F., Quiera F., Queran F., Vonda P., Ken P., Alana P., Anika P., Kare P., Ann B., Chris B., Lauren B., Bonnie B., Walter B., Monica B. and family, Avi M., Dana P., Sean P., Whitney M., Liz B., Mike B., Jeff B., Renee F., Joe F., Tap T., Sopheap T., Ann B., Vonda P.,

Jim H., Debbie H., Jimmy H., Gwen H., John N., Donna N., Joe N., Joshua N., Jason N., James N., Michael Q., Melisa Q., Chris G., Tina G., Joan S., James S., Julie S., Rosh S., Mark S., Maurine S., Arash K., Kian K., Pat G., David G., Cedrick O., Sheila O., Kolab T., Tim T., Brent P., Pat S., Sokhom S., Porlay P., Kealy P., Peter P., Andrew P., Hang P., Abigail P., Steve P., Jordan P., Tyler P., Bailey P., Sohitas R., Hong Z., Tony W., Vonida S., Victory Y., Veng N., Vutha P., Chiv H., Sina S., Wallace S., Jo M., Garry M., Jim M., Debbra P., Madalena L., Scott L., Carrie K., Ken K., Pat G., David G., Brian B., Kathryn B., Brenda R., Brett R., Linda B., David B., Julia H., Joseph H.,

Don J., Bonnie J., Tim M., Eric K., Mary K., Diane M., John M., Eugene P., Carolyn H., Robert H., Nancy G., John G., Spoo D., Tony D., Edward B., Nahid A-F., Linda B., Pat F., Shobha C., Sandeep K., Patty G., Dan G., Lindsay S., Kwame A., Joshua B., Matthew C., Priscilla D., Uma D., Lisa D., Kathy F., Ruben F., Giovanna G., Marina G., Nathan G., Deborah E.,

Mai G., Mekedes K., Fay K., Rita K., Hao L., Sana M., Deneen N., Angie P., Paige J., Heather P., Ben R., Julie R., Davinder R., Graciela R., Jenny S., Molly S., Raymond S., Zomorrod S., Pat S., David T., Julie T., Inyingi U., Tiffiny V., Himanshu B., Honey., Lucy N., James L., Yi Hoen S., Dr., Tran., Borin Y., Karen K., Gulalai J., Kay K., Dao A., Cathleen L., Arthur L., Maiordys M., David T., David M., Dr. Glenna A., James L.,

Yvonne T., Montha O., John O., Amanda O., Brandon O., Evelyne O., Renee O., Vannary T., Vibol T., Cedric T., Daric T., Ravy Y., Hean Y., Virak E., Sakura E., Vira E., Lany H., Bony S., Phat E., Paulie P., Emera P., Clint P., Dawn P., Heather C., Carol M., Bouy T., Rosa T., Mary C., Paula C., Pitou C., Nath C., Chandavy B., Van B., Eric C., Lisa C., Marianne C., Bihn D., Vira H., Chanda K., Michael K., Amrong Y., Tung Y., Regina Y., Sophea K., Khit K., Amanda K., Kok Hong E., Mary Ann K., Very C., Leon C.,

Elizabeth N., Thyya N., Sopheap S., Somany S., Socheata S., Bong Mony S., Bong Ra, Dan S., Sophea S., Bong Srey, Bong Koun, Ra S., Richard L., Channa L., Phanna R., Rithipol., Savary., Ricky, Sinoun S., Somaly S., Chamnan C., Nalen S., Brian S., Stephen S., Megan S., Hong S., Jon S., Nancy, Kevin, Nakry T., Sophia T., Salang B., Saren T., Peou T., Dara S., Pon S., Vannarith N., Thyyan N., Bong Hang, Bong Neang, Linh H., Lany H., Srean L., Tim L., Pauline L., Pov L.

Special thanks to my co-author Monica Boothe and my manager Bonnie Burkhardt who made this book "Two Teaspoons of Rice" possible!

About the Authors

Sida Lei

Sida Lei was born in Cambodia in 1965. She survived as an orphan during the 1975-1979 Khmer Rouge holocaust. Against all odds, she led her siblings in a daring escape to Thailand in 1979. After living in the Thai refugee camps for two years, Sida and her siblings were granted visas to come to the United States. The five Kong children were sponsored by a Catholic family center, Saint Margaret Mary Church, in Rochester New York.

Ms. Lei went on to graduate from the University at Buffalo where she earned a Bachelor of Science in Medical Technology. She wanted a profession where she could give back, help others, and save lives. Sida is happily married to her husband, Jonathan, and has three lovely children: Serena, Sean and Sarah. Ms. Lei currently lives in Fairfax County, Virginia. She works as a clinical microbiologist for the Inova Health System, performing clinical tests for pathogens including the coronavirus COVID-19 Pandemic.

Monica Boothe

A writer of both fiction and nonfiction, Monica earned her MFA in creative writing at George Mason University. She lives in Maryland with her husband, three children, and her cat. She now works at Bowie State University.

Made in the USA
Middletown, DE
20 April 2020